a/85/

American Ingenuity

American

HENRY FORD MUSEUM AND

Original Photography by Ted Spiegel

Ingenuity

GREENFIELD VILLAGE

By James S. Wamsley

Harry N. Abrams, Inc., Publishers, New York

Editor: Joan E. Fisher
Designer: Samuel N. Antupit

Library of Congress Cataloging in Publication Data

Wamsley, James S.
  American ingenuity.
  Includes index.
  1. Henry Ford Museum and Greenfield
Village—Guidebooks. I. Title.
E161.W36 1985 973′.074′017433
84-20435
ISBN 0-8109-0961-8

Pages 2–3. Capturing the essence of the first-flight year of 1903, a one-cylinder Cadillac of that year passes the Greenfield Village home of Orville and Wilbur Wright. Orville helped Henry Ford move the Wright home and shop to Dearborn in 1937. Such early Cadillacs, low-priced and small, were the creation of Henry M. Leland

Title page. The *Torch Lake* is a Mason Fairlie locomotive manufactured by the Mason Fairlie Works of Taunton, Massachusetts, in 1873

Copyright page. This solid-gold presentation trumpet was made in 1866 by Hall and Quinby of Boston for Rhodolph Hall

Right. Proprietary medicine bottles display the labeling and packaging of 1850–60. At left are obverse and reverse of the same product, De Witt's Pain Reliever

Following pages. These nineteenth-century cast-iron toys and banks probably found their first owners in shops much like the Elias Brown General Store, built in Waterford, Michigan, in 1854. Today, its windows overlook The Green of Greenfield Village. With some one hundred structures, the village offers ideal period settings for a wide range of artifacts

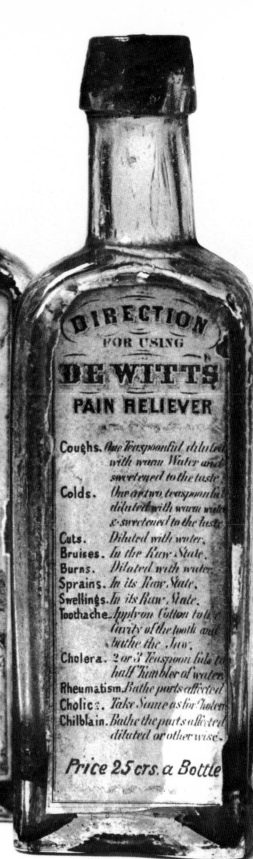

Contents

12 Foreword:
Treasures of
Henry Ford Museum and
Greenfield Village
By Harold K. Skramstad, Jr.

14 Introduction:
Henry Ford's
Amazing
Time Machine

30 The
Quest for
Power

62 The Age of
Noah Webster

102 Lights
Come on at
Menlo Park

152 Triumphs
of Road
and Sky

205 Acknowledgments
and Credits

206 Index

Foreword:

*t*urning the pages of this book is like opening a vast treasure chest of tradition and experience in which every reader can find some rare and valued personal heirlooms.

The Edison Institute—Henry Ford Museum and Greenfield Village—is indeed a treasure, but of a uniquely American kind. Our treasure was not created by kings and hoarded in royal vaults to be seen at a distance by respectful subjects. No, it is one in which we can all share since it represents the common experience of Americans as they worked to build new communities and discovered new ways of doing things that have changed and improved our lives.

It is important to remember this as you explore the wonderful objects of American history that are pictured and described by Jim Wamsley in the following pages. These objects, which delight and inform over a million visitors to Henry Ford Museum and Greenfield Village each year, are important not just in themselves but also in the grand stories they can tell. Grandest of these stories is that of American change. No matter where one looks in our great treasure chest, from carriages to airplanes, from primitive plows to giant reapers, from early printing presses to televisions, these objects reveal with immediacy and eloquent power the ways in which America grew and changed as it moved from the rural, agricultural society of the colonial period to the industrial, urban nation that surrounds us today.

Treasures of Henry Ford Museum and Greenfield Village

It is this large theme of a changing America that guides not only our vast collections but our many educational programs as well. This theme was part of the vision of our founder, Henry Ford, and this book is a reminder that in addition to his industrial innovations he invented a new kind of museum—one that would collect and interpret things not generally associated with traditional museums. Ford recognized early on that the uniqueness of America was to be found in the power of new ideas to shape our lives, so he began a collection of objects and structures which would embody that vision. The result is a museum complex that offers us the new as well as the old, the future as well as the past. To quote Ford, "The farther you look back, the farther you can look ahead."

We at The Edison Institute are constantly at work adding to, preserving, rearranging, and reinterpreting our great historical treasure trove of the American experience to speak in new ways and to tell new stories to new audiences.

This book, rich as it is in both illustrations and text, can show only a small part of the great national treasure that is Henry Ford Museum and Greenfield Village. We invite not only all Americans but all who have an interest in this country to visit us and discover the deep spirit of America that is held here in trust for us all.

Harold K. Skramstad, Jr., *President*
The Edison Institute

Introduction:
Henry Ford's
Amazing
Time Machine

*f*rom the front yard of Noah Webster's Connecticut town house, the eye discerns a plantation home, dozing in its tobacco field, from early Maryland. Shift perspective and encounter the Ontario homestead of Thomas Edison's grandparents, the Massachusetts birthplace of Luther Burbank, and a covered bridge from early Pennsylvania. If you know where to look, and focus patiently beyond the bridge, a new experimental automobile may flicker at high speed across a distant hill. Too far away and moving too fast to reveal a single detail, the silent car, flashing in sunlight on the Ford Motor Company's test track, is more surreal accent than twentieth-century intrusion.

Seen or unseen, the automobile is never far from Greenfield Village or the Henry Ford Museum, which together form The Edison Institute of Dearborn, Michigan. Mr. Ford's stupefying collection of Americana—the world's largest indoor-outdoor museum—initially began with the automobile. The great tycoon's original car, the very keystone of his empire, was itself the first artifact he collected. Ford had built and successfully demonstrated the little Quadricycle in 1896; he then sold it and moved on to newer experimental models. But in 1904, the year he established a new world speed record in one of his cars, he repurchased the Quadricycle for $65. With Ford barely into his forties, his company only a year old, and the first of the marvelous Model Ts four years in the impenetrable future, it was

Opposite. The Ackley Covered Bridge, crossing a stream in Greenfield Village, was originally built in the 1830s above a branch of Wheeling Creek in southwestern Pennsylvania

15

NEW FIRST READER.

LESSON XLI.

bird   rests   gloss-y
come   ri-ses   gold-en
wing   sis-ter   set-tles
           thing pret-ty shi-ning

ee! oh see this shi-ning thing!
rests its gold-en, gloss-y wing:
wing so bright with gold-en light;
, is it not a pret-ty sight?

r, sis-ter, come and see!
not a bird, 'tis not a bee:
ri-ses, up it goes;
set-tles on a rose.

hear   that   aw-ful
haste   then   law-ful
aste   these   arm-ful
gs   those   let-ting
           there   set-ting
           thine   bet-ting

THE ECLECTIC SERIES.   51

LESSON XLII.

meet   mu-sic
woods   be-gun
la-bor   morn-ing
du-ty   mo-ments

The lark is up to meet the sun,
    The bee is on the wing;
The ant its la-bor has be-gun,
    The woods with mu-sic ring.

Shall birds, and bees, and ants, be wise,
    While I my mo-ments waste?
O let me with the morn-ing rise,
    And to my du-ty haste.

fees   goods   why   stick
sees   hoods   who
bees   woods
could   k
woul
shoul

hardly the time for gathering up memories. But already Ford had the instinct for saving that would widen into a collecting passion. He began assembling Edisonia in 1905 and *McGuffey Readers* in 1914. By 1919 he essayed his first building restoration, the old family home at Dearborn, Henry Ford's own birthplace.

The job required removing the building from its original site, where a new highway was about to be constructed, and moving it to new foundations about two hundred feet away. Here began a precise restoration to return it to the condition of the 1870s, when Ford was a child. He even ordered an archeological sifting of the soil, producing such discoveries as his childhood ice skates. It was an exercise in nostalgia in which few people are privileged to indulge, and Ford, as usual, attacked the project with fervor. He personally searched from rural Michigan to New England until he found a duplicate of the 1867 Starlight stove that once warmed the Fords's parlor.

About the same time he began the homestead restoration, Ford became the center of a newspaper tempest in which he was ridiculed as an ignoramus who believed "history was bunk." The point he *had* been trying to make, and which had inadvertently stoked the adverse publicity, was that orthodox history dealt with politics, wars, and treaties, and that historians actually knew—or taught—precious little about how the people of vanished eras actually lived. Ford began forming the idea of a museum of industrial history that would help correct the imbalance. By 1922, his preliminary collecting of tools and machines had broadened to include the totality of American antiques. He was hooked. In 1924 came an exercise that expanded Ford's interest in historic restoration and fine antiques as well: he bought the historic Wayside Inn in South Sudbury, Massachusetts. Soon he was devoting as much as two days per week to collecting, and boxcar loads of antiques started arriving at the Ford industrial complex in Dearborn for storage in a former tractor plant. "We have no Egyptian mummies here, nor any relics of the Battle of Waterloo, nor do we have any curios from Pompeii, for everything we have is strictly American," Ford said. The claim would not prove to be literally true, but Henry did hew to an overwhelmingly American theme. American craftsmanship, inventiveness, engineering, and work habits never had a better champion.

In about 1926 Ford conceived the idea for a two-part "Edison Institute" at Dearborn. A great museum would display the artifacts of American culture, and out the door a village would preserve the community setting of long ago. Pushed along by Ford's relentless energy and stupendous resources, matters moved quickly. The first old building, a general store, arrived at Dearborn in 1927, and he made a key decision: to reconstruct a cluster of buildings central to the career of Thomas Alva Edison, including a significant portion of the famous Edison research and development facility from Menlo Park, New Jersey.

Edison, who was still alive and in relatively good health, journeyed to

Opposite. William Holmes McGuffey, author of *McGuffey's Eclectic Readers*, was born in 1800 in this one-room log cabin, originally located in Washington County, Pennsylvania

New Jersey with Ford to inspect what remained of the Menlo Park lab. A photograph of the event captures the blade-slim Ford, neatly dressed as always, and Edison, in an equally characteristic state of dishevelment, standing in the ruins of the laboratory as Ford was bellowing something into the ear of the deaf old genius. Most of the buildings had vanished, but Ford obtained the original Sarah Jordan boarding house, where many of Edison's crew had lived, plus a small building where the first glass lightbulbs were blown. He also retrieved tons of fragmented materials, including original boards and bricks, fused masses of buried debris (such as broken bottles, crucibles, and experimental wiring), and the rotted stump of a tree where Edison once tied a pet bear. More than a dozen rail cars filled with the red clay that surrounded the buildings were sent. A former Edison assistant, Francis Jehl, agreed to come to Greenfield Village to direct the reconstruction. In September 1928, Edison came to Dearborn to inspect the completion of another of his reincarnated laboratories, the long-time winter headquarters in Fort Myers, Florida. Construction was beginning on the new museum building that would adjoin the village, and at Ford's bidding Edison plunged the spade of the late Luther Burbank into a cube of wet cement. Then the old inventor scratched his name deeply into the surface.

One year later, on October 21, 1929, Edison returned for the dedication of the Edison Institute, a star-studded event fixed by Ford to coincide with the fiftieth anniversary of the invention of incandescent lighting. Henry spared no expense and ignored no detail. To carry Mr. and Mrs. Edison, President and Mrs. Herbert Hoover, and Mrs. Ford and himself the last few miles to Greenfield Village, a mid-nineteenth-century train was newly restored to duplicate one on which Edison had served as a newsboy. Steaming to the village, the passengers dismounted at the very railroad station—moved from Smiths Creek, Michigan—where Edison had once been ejected from the train for setting it on fire. The guests for the events that evening included Orville Wright, Madame Eve Curie, John D. Rockefeller, Jr., and Will Rogers, who would say afterward that he was disappointed: "I thought they would give out Lincolns as souvenirs. Shoot, they didn't even pass around Fords."

Edison and Francis Jehl had the previous day made a duplicate of the first successful lightbulb, and after dinner Ford and President Hoover joined the two scientists in the upstairs Menlo Park laboratory for a reenactment of the event of fifty years before. Pioneer NBC radio newsman Graham McNamee, broadcasting from the scene, barked the description in his then-familiar staccato: "Mr. Edison has the two wires in his hand; now he is reaching up to the old lamp; now he is making the connection. It lights!" In a prearranged, elaborate national ceremony, lights switched on, bells pealed, and horns sounded.

The grand evening would always be the key event in the particular history of the museum and village. "Think of it," said Harold K. Skramstad,

Opposite. A full complement of horse-drawn vehicles enhances the Greenfield Village scene, and some—such as the yellow omnibus—are used for visitor sightseeing

Above. Philadelphia's Independence Hall was copied for the façade of the Henry Ford Museum, and the structure's central tower became the chief landmark of The Edison Institute. Behind the Georgian front, most of the vast museum followed the lines of Ford's factory buildings of the late 1920s

Opposite. Mrs. Daniel Cohen operated her Detroit store in the late nineteenth century. Moved to Greenfield Village, the shop actively interprets a typical city millinery of the time, demonstrating clothing and accessory styles, retail techniques, the distribution of manufactured goods, and the success of women in trade, all at a time approximating the critical years of the Wright brothers, whose shop is across the street

Jr., president of Edison Institute in 1984, "how many times can you get the same people back for a dedication fifty years later? It was like getting George Washington back to re-create crossing the Delaware."

It was also the last national extravaganza of unalloyed happiness in the 1920s. In less than one week the stock market crashed and the nation began to sink into the Great Depression. Edison died less than two years later, eulogized by Henry Ford as a great man who changed the world, and whose every work was beneficial to mankind. "Mr. Edison himself did not grow old. He was like a young driver in a worn-out car. He has just gone, I believe, to get new facilities to continue his work. But the sense of personal loss is very heavy. There was only one Edison."

Ford had revered Edison as a boyhood idol and gone on to know him for nearly forty years. But other Americans amply filled the car maker's requirements for enshrinement in his village, and he sought their relics also and, if possible, some associated structure. Webster's house was already being razed in New Haven, Connecticut, when Ford learned about it and dispatched experts for a hairbreadth rescue. He obtained the log cabin birthplace of his educational hero, William Holmes McGuffey, and a former courthouse from Illinois where young Abraham Lincoln practiced law. Ford even rebuilt the one-room schoolhouse where he received his own short, but cherished, formal education. The Wright brothers' home and shop, moved to the village with the assistance of Orville Wright himself, ranked with the Menlo Park complex in significance, and were of greater originality. Some buildings, such as the brick home where H.J. Heinz created the first of his varieties, were added after Ford's death.

The presence of the buildings and relics associated with such famous Americans does create, inevitably, a pantheonic aspect which under other circumstances might have been overpowering but which is subdued by several restraints. One is implicit in the sorts of people Henry Ford admired, whether renowned or humble: practical problem-solvers, men of plain speech and hard work, with generally low quotients of pretension and cant. The ghosts of Thomas Edison, George Washington Carver, or the Wrights are more inclined to appear in work clothes than in radiant togas. Moreover, there are not all that many famous names among the Greenfield Village shades. The former occupants of these hundred-odd buildings tended to be the middling kind, such as innkeeper Calvin Wood of the restored and lively Eagle Tavern, or Mrs. D. Cohen of the millinery shop, or a smudgy legion of nameless machinists, blacksmiths, and millers.

The village's complex interpretive program, spanning four centuries, puts its emphasis squarely on the changing lives of ordinary Americans while keeping the famous in healthy perspective. The courthouse where Abraham Lincoln practiced law is no longer presented as a shrine of Lincoln memorabilia, which was as riveting—and as distracting—as a spotlight. Now it is interpreted as a community's heart of legal and government

action. Such changes in village tradition can create unexpected reactions among visitors. The curatorial staff was asked, in effect, how dare it de-Lincolnize the Logan County Courthouse?

More and more, Greenfield Village is perceived by the public as a living community with its own sanctified traditions. A few visitors have come regularly for more than fifty years, a period longer than the span from Edison's first bulb to the great re-creation in 1929. People who came as children in the 1930s and '40s now bring their grandchildren. For such champions the village becomes a sort of hometown of the soul. President Skramstad is convinced that such visitors develop a sense of proprietorship about the village and museum. "One buys into the whole American experience here. It is a surrogate for owning historical objects. Unfortunately, when we make changes we're violating history as far as they're concerned. Still, the concept of the *possession* of history here is one of our greatest strengths."

Some of Ford's prejudices showed through in his disposition of the village, as when he decreed three clock and watch shops (reduced now to one) but no banks. Regionally, the buildings and exhibits heavily favor the northeast quarter of the United States. Yet such a basic range of American life spreads across these cunning 240 acres that no visitor can depart without a better understanding of the massive changes lived through by our ancestors.

The last building to be moved to the village in Ford's lifetime was, strangely, the first one he restored: the family farm. After moving safely from the highway's path, the house had served through the 1920s and '30s as an occasional social retreat for Henry and Clara Ford and their friends. Donning period costumes, the group gamboled through American country dances under the direction of Ford's private dancing master, for the tycoon unabashedly enjoyed the music and steps of America's past. Finally, in 1944, the old man decided the time had come to gather his birthplace into the American town of his dreams.

Greenfield Village, through its human scale, skilled interpretation, and undeniable charm, speaks in a different vocabulary from that of the Ford Museum next door. There, the full force of Henry Ford's collecting fever reveals itself indoors across twelve acres of artifacts. Many of the collections are the world's best and largest. Automobiles, furniture, watches and clocks, agricultural implements, musical instruments, communications devices, lighting, power equipment, ceramics, glass, metals, domestic appliances of every kind are deployed to the horizon.

Ford backed his omniverous collecting with vast wealth and his far-flung organization of clever and resourceful staff, many of them with engineering or mechanical skills. Thus Herbert F. Morton, an English engineer, was able to comb the British Isles for such rarities as the museum's eighteenth-century Newcomen steam engine from England. Most of the objects Ford collected were American, however, and dated after 1800, with the greatest

Above and opposite. The Eagle Tavern was built in the 1830s at Clinton, Michigan, and served stagecoach passengers on the Detroit–Chicago road. Moved to Greenfield Village, the Eagle Tavern again approximates its years of pre-Civil War hospitality. "Living History" interpreters serve period food and beverages in a lively setting

strength in the years from 1850 to the very early 1900s. The collections therefore fall naturally through the peak years of America's technological and social change as we moved from the traditional, agricultural society of the eighteenth century to the urbanized, technological world that endures today. No better exhibit on the Industrial Revolution can be found, but the Ford collections go beyond technology to address the entire subject of changing America.

Henry Ford's viewpoint on those changes was altogether positive; he believed that innovation and technology would lead inevitably to a better future. As one of the world's mightiest influences for change, having done more than anyone else to give mobility to the average person, Ford is often pictured as concerned by the rapidity with which his works were altering the face of older, more traditional America. That might explain some of his interest in old buildings. Much of what he collected was, at the time, of no such significance, but merely twenty- to fifty-year-old merchandise: obsolete stoves, carpet sweepers, milk bottles, steam engines, reapers, printing presses. It was an astonishing performance. Only a few others were collecting such things. While other wealthy men indulged themselves by amassing works by French Impressionists, Ford—at least one side of Ford—gathered "the common objects, the things that bound us together, rather than the things that separated us," in Skramstad's description.

Another side of the tycoon, however, went straight for the finest traditional, pre-Industrial Revolution furniture and decorative arts. That, too, was remarkable, for the 1920s was a pioneering time for major antiques collecting, before the days of Winterthur and Colonial Williamsburg. American antique furniture was not as coveted as it is today, and little was known about it. Ford received rock-solid help from a visionary antiques dealer, Israel Sack, of Boston and later of New York. Ford bought many of the best antiques from the Sack firm for decades, but initially there were awkward moments, as recalled by Harold Sack, son of Israel. Henry Ford ordered his staff to strip the old finish and apply shiny new varnish on his acquisitions, even on a piece in good original condition. "He started to refinish things, and my father told him, 'Don't you do that.' His secretary said, 'Don't talk to Mr. Ford like that. Nobody talks to Mr. Ford like that.' My father said, 'He's taking off one hundred and fifty years of patina; I'm telling him.' And so he stopped."

Harold Sack recalled Ford's many trips to the Sack establishment early in the 1930s. "Every time he came into the store, he'd come up and grab my eyelid, pull it down, look close, and say, 'Well, young fellow, I see you're leading a clean life.' Then he'd go around and stick his head in all the clocks. He opened up the clock doors and looked in. He had a very small head, but I was sure he was going to get his head stuck ... Henry Ford and my father became very good friends. They used to race together. They'd run footraces. It was a different era, a time when collectors and dealers were people-to-people."

The scope of Ford's collections challenges the museum staff to produce meaningful interpretive techniques. Ford believed that almost any artifact could be read like a book, conveying its story to anyone taking the time to study it. He was personally familiar with much of what he collected. Later generations of the public would not understand what they were seeing. These days, the pleased cry of "Look there, we had one of those," is heard less often in the galleries. For each generation, the need is to convey the meaning and excitement of certain key artifacts, even introducing the viewer to entirely new vocabularies and systems of thought. On the other hand, collectors—whose enthusiasms are already fixed and stimulated, whether for old radios, cars, furniture, or whatever—want to see as many artifacts as possible crammed into the smallest space. "If we're to do our job well, history must speak to a large audience," Harold Skramstad says, "and we have to make people aware that whether they've thought about it or not, they live in a world that was a result of this transformation."

With collections spanning four centuries and ranging from masterpieces of Queen Anne furniture to a power plant from Henry Ford's main Model T factory, the interpretive techniques vary. There isn't much that can be done with the mammoth Highland Park factory generator of 1912 but let it sit there. Some artifacts seem to have their own ad hoc existence on an exclusive plane, such as the Indian spinning wheel presented to Henry Ford (in an exchange of mutual admiration) by Mohandas K. Gandhi, or George Washington's portable camp bed from the Revolutionary War. In other areas the broader stories emerge majestically. One of the most successful, the museum's big chronological display of furniture masterpieces, creates a sense of heightened awareness not possible in period settings. It is the sort of exhibit that Ford himself might have loved: rich, encyclopedic, not gussied up with artifice.

Ford never threw anything away, and the written records of his long career, plus the documents of his world-wide manufacturing empire, piled up in a dense mass. Meanwhile, he became interested in collecting rare books and documents, a logical extension of his original trove of *McGuffey Readers.* The Edison Institute's combined archives and research library today holds (in addition to Henry's original 250 different *McGuffeys*) thousands of rare books, including more than fifty *New England Primers,* the first English Bible printed in America, and such later rarities as a first edition *Wizard of Oz.* While emphasis is on American imprints, the library has two sets of Diderot's *Encyclopédie.*

Priceless as such items may be, books are nevertheless easier to comprehend as artifacts than the institute's holdings in still more exotic ephemera. Consider a group of some three thousand trade catalogues, mostly of the nineteenth century, with related gatherings of posters, trade cards, and advertisements, together forming a core study of the early history of American advertising. Add thousands of old almanacs, complete files of once-

prominent periodicals, hundreds of yellowed broadsides, about one thousand Currier and Ives lithographs. The music collection includes a complete file of Stephen Foster's first editions. The map collection, beginning with the sixteenth century, includes the supremely important 1755 John Mitchell plan of North America used at the Treaty of Paris negotiations ending the Revolutionary War. Less glamorous, but perhaps no less important, are tons of business and personal records from, among others, Edison, H. J. Heinz, the Boston & Sandwich Glass Company, and the Wright brothers. And, of course, the incomparable records of Henry Ford and his company.

"We're going to start something," he said in 1919. "I'm going to start up a museum and give people a true picture of the development of the country." He also promised that "When we are through, we shall have reproduced American life as lived." Building a perfect time machine was too great a task even for Henry Ford, but no one ever made a nobler effort, and it is fairly certain that no one ever will. How well did he succeed? In the case of one visitor, at least, perhaps too well. On departing Greenfield Village he wrote on a visitor's comment card: "I never knew that Henry Ford, Thomas Edison, and the Wright brothers all lived on the same street."

They didn't, of course. And yet they did.

Sometimes, the Brobdingnagian scope of the institute's properties can be downright overwhelming to a visitor. What are we to make of these endless ranks of artifacts? What is the message of all these silent survivors of untold years, vanished processes, forgotten needs, and long-solved problems? The questions are those common to historical museums everywhere, but here they assume heroic proportions.

Take the cars. Gleaming like Greek pastry, row on row, they are safe now from the infinity of hazards that claimed their brethren. The primitive Packard that won the great transcontinental race of 1903 bears no scars from its mighty exertions, for it has been restored at least twice. As perfect, too, are all the perky Model Ts, the various editions that put America on wheels across a span of less than twenty years. We search the shiny flanks of assorted Overlands, Stutzes, and Marmons for clues to the reality of highway travel in the 1920s. But we cannot really imagine the struggles they encountered—the boglike roads, incessant flat tires, and scarce and incompetent service. The closest we see is out on the streets of Greenfield Village, where chuckling along with a load of tourists is a Model T touring car, its black enamel lightly smudged by curious, friendly hands.

Well, what do we expect? Hazards lie in seeking too much from interpretive support. Interpretation has practical limits, and it can even invoke counterproductive reactions. "Living History," where staff actors take parts ranging from New England colonials to 1850ish tavern servers, is presented in Greenfield Village. Most visitors like it, yet some consider it gimmickry for the multitude. Such a division merely underlines one of the potential

Opposite. The Grimm Jewelry Shop was owned and operated by Engelberg Grimm from 1886 to 1930; ten years later it was moved from Michigan Avenue in Detroit to Greenfield Village, with much of its inventory intact

conflicts of historical museums: the misalliance of a few consecrated scholars and experts, and the cursory public swarm.

The latter class wants to enjoy itself, but here it seems surprisingly knowledgeable, too. Along the museum aisles at any given moment, dozens of elderly men are explaining to their grandchildren the arcane mysteries of beveled gears and poppet valves, the force of compound levers, and the production miracles of 1947; grandmothers are exclaiming as they recognize and remember—not always fondly—laundry wringers, parlor organs, and flour bins like the ones in their mothers' kitchen cabinets. Such universal reactions often seem etched in dignity and pathos.

Taken all together, the museum's collections create a sort of cosmic electrical grid of the American domestic and industrial past. Visitors may discover that they are already part of the circuit, or they may find points where they can plug in. But, inevitably, as the years pass, the factor of a visitor's personal recollection is of ever-diminishing importance. As each generation gives way to another, the artifacts it remembered from its youth pass from nostalgia into history. Few people today can recall a factory-fresh Model T or a new kitchen cabinet with a flour dispenser.

If there is a single theme resounding through this amazing treasury, it is change in American life. Nowhere else can we trace it so completely. Here we view homes and furnishings from the 1600s to the 1900s. We see our forebears' shops, power sources, inventions, products, and diversions. We learn how we fed ourselves. We perceive the awesome force of the Industrial Revolution. All of that is here and, even if it sometimes appears too vast and confusing to grasp, a majestic chronology is present, too. The following chapters seek to illuminate that chronology, by relating selected museum and village exhibits to their places in the national past, and by exploring some of their interlocking roles. We are embarking on a walk through history, with a cast of five-star artifacts guiding the way.

The
Quest
for
Power

*b*y the final decade of the seventeenth century, Great Britain was wresting world financial leadership from the Dutch with a new banking structure and a quick-rising society of capitalist entrepreneurs. Abundant natural resources flowed in from the empire's far-flung dominions. The labor pool was large and capable. Growth and the profit motive received the blessings of government. A traditional country of agriculture, trade, and crafts was about to begin the boundless innovative cycle that would change the world forever.

Not only did eighteenth-century Britain give birth to the Industrial Revolution, she would be transformed by it far faster and more completely than her other old rival across the English Channel, France. Britain's new, fluid economy stimulated and rewarded inventiveness. France, topheavy from its huge royal, aristocratic, and clerical superstructure, had a different viewpoint on the profit motive. Furthermore, Britain had already gained the edge in commercial warfare and thus owned a wider trading universe than France.

Yet, for all that, the irrepressible French genius for invention made its mark at key points. Nothing could be more crucial to the Industrial Revolution than the steam engine, and a French mathematics professor, Denis Papin, may have been present at the creation. After performing significant experiments in the influence of atmospheric pressure on boiling points,

Papin designed, in 1690, a steam-operated, piston-driven pump. He may have even tried to build a steamboat.

By 1698, steam was up in an English boiler, built by Thomas Savery. But Savery's big effort failed because the boiler could not stand the pressure. The honor of bringing forth the world's first commercially successful steam engine would fall upon Englishman Thomas Newcomen, around 1711, sharing Savery's patent. Newcomen, an iron merchant from Dartmouth, was a little-known figure despite his incalculable legacy. His engines went straight to work, pumping the vexatious water from English coal mines.

Having set free the genie of power, Newcomen died in 1729, but his engines worked so well that others continued building them. Around 1750, an unknown maker installed a Newcomen at a colliery in Lancashire's Fairbottom Valley. Until 1827, when the mine closed, the big pump's eighteen-foot-long rocking beam nodded back and forth on its tall, cut-stone base, pumping fourteen strokes per minute from a depth of 240 feet. Then the pump sat unused for more than a century until the Earl of Stamford presented it to Henry Ford in 1929, exactly two hundred years after Newcomen died. Re-erected in the Ford Museum, the ancient machine looks for all the world like today's automatic oil field pumps. But its pitted, massive iron fittings and original stone mounting are clear testimony to its antiquity. It is believed to be the oldest such engine in existence. The venerable Newcomen is, perhaps, the primal relic of the Industrial Revolution.

James Watt, the man who usually gets the credit for the invention of the steam engine, was a University of Glasgow instrument maker. In repairing a teaching model of a Newcomen engine, Watt perceived the route to some important improvements, and by 1765 he invented the separate condensing chamber and air pump. Technically, Newcomen's engine was "atmospheric," with its power stroke assisted by atmospheric pressure.

Watt received the financial backing of wealthy merchant Matthew Boulton in 1774, and the new firm of Boulton and Watt set about building engines. In 1796 they established a new power plant for the Warwick and Birmingham Canal Navigation Company in Birmingham, England, where it pumped water to locks on the Bordesley Canal until it was judged obsolete and retired in 1854, although it could still lift 134,000 gallons of water per hour with its giant, ninety-six-inch stroke. Ford obtained the engine in 1929 from its original foundations; at Dearborn, joined by other Watt-type engines and the incomparable Newcomen, it completes a rare glimpse into the dawn of the age of steam.

Fully as important as Watt's other innovations was his success, early in the 1780s, in adapting his engines to deliver rotary motion. Thus appeared for the first time the principles of planetary crank, rotating flywheel, and speed-controlling governor. Such a breakthrough meant that steam could at last be harnessed to factory equipment. Until then, the basic power source of textile mills—in many ways the leading edge of the Industrial

Opposite. These rare examples of steam-power equipment are primal relics of the Industrial Revolution. In the foreground, the round device of riveted plates is a "haystack" boiler of c. 1780; behind it stands the tilted beam of Fairbottom Bobs, a Newcomen-type engine that successfully pumped water from English coal mines. Dating from about 1760, it is the senior entry in the Ford Museum's large collection of steam engines

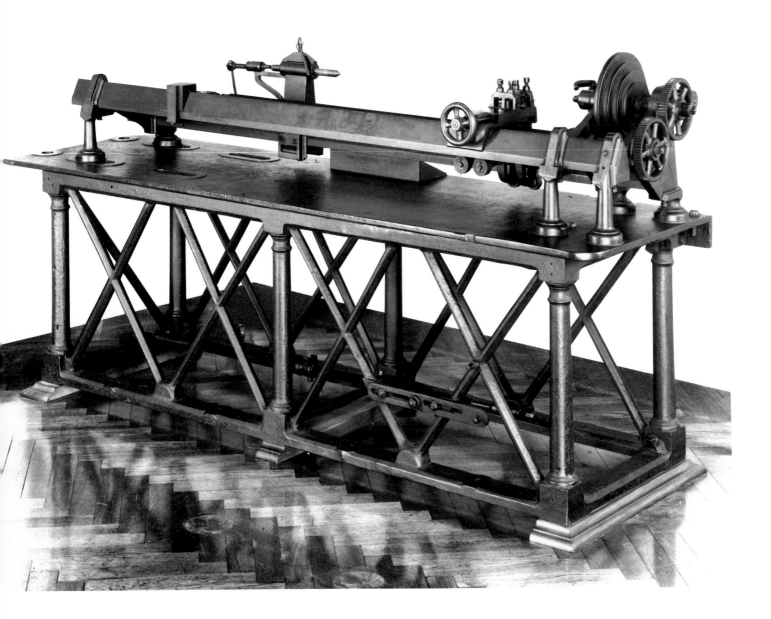

Revolution—was water power, which worked reasonably well but always carried its own built-in geographical restraint.

The textile industry had advanced quickly since John Kay invented in 1733 the "flying shuttle," which trebled a loom's production. In 1769 Richard Arkwright invented the first water-powered spinning machine, the water frame, and Edmund Cartwright unveiled the power loom in 1785. With such mechanized assistance, unheard-of fabric production flowed through the hands of cheap, semiskilled labor. A clever British textile engineer, Samuel Slater, migrated to the United States in 1789 and founded the modern American textile industry, at Pawtucket, Rhode Island.

Slater's Mill was powered by water, but the earliest mills in the American colonies were powered by wind. Some were patterned after the post mills developed in twelfth-century Germany; other colonial millwrights adopted the Netherlands style of tower mills. Both were equally subject to the wind's maddening capriciousness. In the middle 1600s, a tower gristmill was erected at West Yarmouth, Massachusetts, and it somehow survived not only the hazards of time but also those of at least three moves to more promising locations. Henry Ford moved it again, for the last time, to Greenfield Village.

Millers and spinners may have had power, but there was precious little power for the bench craftsman of the seventeenth and eighteenth centuries. One partial exception was the lathe, which had been around for thousands of years and could be turned by a foot treadle, a big hand-cranked flywheel, or—very rarely—by a water wheel. Original lathes of the preindustrial era are rare indeed, but the museum displays a big one that was probably built in America about 1775, and was used for turning such major items as bedposts and newel posts as long as seventy-two inches. The treadle-powered lathe was not for the weak of leg: its operator pumped power to a fifty-four-inch-diameter pulley that spun the headstock. Built primarily of wood, the brawny old machine was reinforced at key points with heavy iron fittings.

Later in the eighteenth century, as the steam engine proved its mettle, perceptive engineers and manufacturers grasped the potential of power-driven equipment of greater size and complexity than anyone had ever seen. Before that could occur, however, came the matter of making machines to build such paragons. A world lacking in machines had to create an entire machine tool industry before getting on with the Industrial Revolution, and the required leadership emerged in England's first generation of tool engineers. In 1775, John Wilkinson devised a boring mill to produce steam engine cylinders of unprecedented accuracy. Henry Maudslay worked developmental miracles on metalworking lathes, and was a primary influence on Western machine tool development and standardized precision manufacture. A Maudslay pupil, Joseph Whitworth, is still better known: he left his name on a measurement system enduring to our own time, and became the leading machine tool builder of the early nineteenth century. Representing

Opposite. About the beginning of the nineteenth century, English designers and craftsmen made rapid headway in producing tools of such precision and reliability as never seen before. Without such equipment as this screw-cutting metal lathe of about 1828, the Industrial Revolution could not have developed as it did. This rare, beautifully designed lathe was probably made by pioneer toolmaker Joseph Whitworth at the works of Maudslay, Sons and Field

Whitworth's great work is a metal-turning lathe of 1828, not only a superbly functioning machine tool but a lovely specimen of classical revival design. Its key role was to make parts for *other* lathes.

The quest to harness electricity would prove infinitely more difficult than bridling steam. The effort began early: Queen Elizabeth's court physician released a scholarly study on electricity in 1600, a pioneering work for which Dr. William Gilbert is sometimes called the "father of modern electricity." Generations of patient, earnest, usually bewildered successors added their layers of work, much of it, such as the discovery of the Leyden jar, represented or demonstrated in museum displays. When Pieter van Musschenbroek captured current in a jar at the University of Leyden in 1746, the results were sensational. Electricity was provocative and mysterious. Benjamin Franklin was among those fascinated by Leyden jars, and his consequent experiments produced original data on positive and negative charges, or polarity. Another key piece of eighteenth-century equipment was the electrostatic generator, followed by Alessandro Volta's invention of the electrochemical battery in 1800.

Despite such straws in the wind, eighteenth-century life remained essentially traditional, preserving many ancient unsolved problems. Consider the plow. There it stands, a museum exhibit, gnawed by years and use, the very symbol of tillage. We can afford to be sentimental about it, for no longer is the plow an instrument of arduous toil and frustration. We can sympathize with the forgotten millions of plowmen who trudged endlessly along their clodded furrows, yanking reins and clutching handles behind teams of heaving oxen.

The plow, it turns out, was always inadequate for the task. Mankind's ingenuity came late to the farm, a lapse not wholly explained by cheap labor and imperfect metallurgy. We had reached the 1700s before English and Low Country agriculturists interested themselves in improving the design of plows and produced a new model with a curved wooden moldboard.

Colonial America made almost as many variants as there were local blacksmiths and wheelwrights, the traditional makers of plows. Even the great Thomas Jefferson, enthusing that "the plough is to the farmer what the wand is to the sorcerer," tried his hand at designing a scientific moldboard that would slip easily through the soil. Predictably, Jefferson's mathematics were correct and his sense of design impeccable, but as a practical matter his plow was too exacting for the day's unreliable, or inconsistent, technology of handcrafted wood and iron. The French Society of Agriculture presented him with a gold medal for his creation, but farmers would have to wait for the Industrial Revolution to catch up with Mr. Jefferson. Today, the museum's collection of eighteenth-century plows—including "barshare" specimens from New England and Pennsylvania and a Dutch or "hog" plow from New York—silently recall the tillers' years of struggle.

Rarer, even, than plows are surviving eighteenth-century vehicles. Built

Opposite. Any American-built vehicle of the eighteenth century is exceptionally rare, and the museum displays one of the best—a 1797 "chariot." Built by William Ross of New York City for Angelica Campbell of Schenectady, New York, the handcrafted masterpiece somehow survived the wretched roads of its time

largely of wood, they shook apart and rotted out with distressing rapidity. The exceptions were Europe's ornate carriages built for nobility: such rigs were more prone to be sheltered, and the finest were saved for important state occasions. Thus a good rate of survival preserved some of the most ornate vehicles, but almost none remain from everyday life.

Compared to Europe, America had relatively few passenger vehicles of any kind. The great distances within and between the colonies and the poor condition of streets and highways rendered carriages generally impractical save for a few urban areas. The aristocracy owned them, but as a practical matter their use was limited. Horseback travel was quicker and more efficient. Two-wheeled carts called "riding chairs," designed to carry the driver in lonely prominence, were a popular alternative. Two wheels were often better than four in negotiating wretched roads, but "chairs" were uncomfortable and prone to pitch the occupant out in even minor mishaps.

A rare example of the high level of work to which American coachbuilders could rise is a museum vehicle dating from about 1797. Called in its day a "chariot," such a four-wheeled carriage would later be called a "coupe" for its short, half-coach configuration, with one forward-facing seat inside. The chariot was light, maneuverable, and could be ventilated in hot weather by lowering its front windows, the distant ancestors of a car's windshield. Built with wonderful skill and sophistication by William Ross of New York City, the chariot was originally owned by Angelica Campbell of Schenectady, whose initials still are emblazoned with coats of arms on the faded black exterior. With silver handles on the doors, and carpeted folding steps, the elegant chariot welcomed riders to a plush interior of tufted buff fabric, accented by red leather, and needlepointed window pulls in red, gold, and white. Even the coachman's lofty seat was ornamented by a handsome needlepoint hammercloth, and the footman—who rode behind—cushioned his feet on a padded leather platform while he clutched needlepointed hand straps as the chariot jolted along Schenectady's streets in the last years of the eighteenth century.

Some potent alchemy must have been present in the Conestoga River Valley of Pennsylvania between 1725 and 1750, when the Lancaster County region gave birth to two of the most American of all designs: the long rifle and the Conestoga wagon. The graceful Conestoga evolved from nothing more grand than a German farm wagon, and indeed the earliest versions were used to carry farm produce into colonial cities. As settlement proceeded west, so did the rugged Conestogas, hauling freight across the mountains to Pittsburgh, and down the Shenandoah Valley from Philadelphia and Baltimore. Usually drawn by bell-decked six-horse teams, the wagons carried up to eight tons of payload. Their characteristic curved bottoms, rising at each end, kept the loads from shifting and thus reduced strain on the endgates. Massive, dished, twelve- and sixteen-spoke wheels bore the gross burden, while the driver had several options of position: he

could rest on the lazyboard projecting from the left side; he could ride the left wheel horse; or he could walk alongside. Never did he ride inside or up front behind the horses. Americans drive on the right side of the road today, from a position on their vehicles' left, because, legend says, the example was set by those vanished teamsters.

The museum's Conestoga wagon is a beautiful, original example with body of faded powder blue; the running gear is a still-more-faded red. Its ironwork does not exhibit quite the ornamental artistry that made some wagons into showcases for the blacksmith's craft, perhaps because it came relatively late in the period. Dating between 1810 and 1840, this grand survivor of a colorful epoch could, like its brethren, overcome almost any hazard but one: arrival of the railroad. When the iron horse crossed the Alleghenies, the great wagons' work was done. Later, a substantially modified descendant would become the prairie schooner of the American West.

*i*t is well that "Pilgrim" furniture is so homely; otherwise we might grow too fond of it and discover how unavailable are specimens of seventeenth-century furniture. American-made pieces of the era have become so rare and costly as to be largely confined to museum collections, where we can study them across the void of time, with interest but usually without covetousness. The museum's large collection of seventeenth-century American furniture is heavily New England in origin, and includes Brewster and Carver chairs bristling with bulbously turned spindles; awkward-looking hard stools; cupboards and chests festooned with pointless balusters, bosses, and drop finials, and covered with complex but crude geometric carvings. The wonder is that such styles persisted to the very dawn of the eighteenth century; that New Englanders for so long repeated the old country's medieval and Renaissance traditions. And why favor oak, that most difficult wood to work by hand, when the forests were crying with better alternatives?

Yet the design of some seventeenth-century furniture made sense. Americans did not have nearly as much furniture then, and they were often cramped for space as well. Multipurpose furniture thus was useful. The museum's exceptionally rare chair-table combination from Massachusetts, c. 1650, is one of America's earliest-known space-savers. It still has its original drawer and, even more unusual, much of its original dark red paint. From a bit later, about 1690, comes a boxy chest-over-drawer of the Connecticut River Valley of Massachusetts, its front chiseled with tulips, leaves, and scrolls, and even the initials of the long-departed original owner, Maria Wheelock. This striking design is often termed a Hadley chest.

A strange and welcome development occurred around the end of the seventeenth century: coincident with the advent of the new and more elegant style of William and Mary, the skill standards of American furniture crafts-

Opposite. The museum's collection of American furniture, remarkable for completeness and quality, is among the nation's very best. This rare oak chair-table, made in Massachusetts in the mid-1600s, was useful as a space saver in the era's frequently small, crowded homes

Above. Two rare chairs from early New England display contrasting forms. The oak armchair at top, from eastern Massachusetts, dates from 1650–80. The New England maple armchair below originated in 1700–25

men made a giant leap forward. With surprising speed, craftsmen refined their techniques to accommodate the new designs. A prime example is the museum's high chest (or highboy) that once belonged to George Washington's mother, a Virginia plantation matron. With drawers faced in two types of walnut veneer, six trumpet-turned legs, curving stretchers, and brass fittings, the Washington highboy seems light-years away from its Pilgrim-era predecessors. The piece, attributed to New England despite its provenance, has a secondary history. Exhibited at the enormously influential World's Columbian Exposition at Chicago in 1893, it stimulated a new interest in American antiquarianism.

The William and Mary style did not last long, but did its work as a technical and artistic bridge to the still more graceful design school of Queen Anne. The museum's many examples indicate the range of artistry and style already introduced by 1730. One from that date, a linen press attributed to Ebenezer Hartshorne of Charlestown, Massachusetts, is constructed of walnut with rosewood and satinwood inlays. Reeded columns, arch-top doors, broken-arch bonnet and urn finial, butterfly brasses: many of the lineaments of the balance of the eighteenth century were firmly in place. An important cherry desk and bookcase of about 1730, probably from Connecticut, is beautifully carved with corkscrew finials, shells, and flowers. Queen Anne chairs are coveted by collectors; the museum's collection illustrates their variety.

The ensuing Chippendale period was, to many lovers of antique furniture, epitomized in the famed Philadelphia highboy, or high chest of drawers. Some experts believe that at least a few examples of the breed were excessively large and showy. A possible example of the latter category is an eight-foot-one-inch-tall walnut specimen with applied tendrils of carved wooden leafage crawling top and bottom. Nearby, more restrained examples of this great American classic allow the viewer to make up his own mind. Philadelphia indeed was one of America's polestars of fine eighteenth-century furniture. Among its practitioners was Thomas Affleck, who made furniture in the Chippendale style for the U.S. Supreme Court in 1790, when the court sat in Philadelphia. The museum displays a chair from that chamber along with other Affleck work, including an elegant card table from 1765–80.

Another major Chippendale piece is the mahogany blockfront desk of about 1770 to 1800, attributed to Samuel Loomis of Colchester, Connecticut. Its design, of block and shell slant top and three blocked drawers, seems incapable of improvement; the execution displays the mastery that American craftsmen had long since achieved. Such pieces could be afforded only by the wealthy few; a 1785 middle-class success story would more likely have been marked by such acquisitions as the museum's well-made Windsor chair of hickory, maple, and pine, still bearing its original buff paint with black trim.

Above. The style change from Queen Anne to Chippendale seems epitomized by these two Philadelphia armchairs. The Queen Anne chair (top), with solid fiddleback splat, dates from about 1750 and is made of walnut. Contrast it with the open carved mahogany back of the Chippendale-style chair (bottom) that replaced it in popularity, starting about 1755

Opposite. The grace of American Chippendale shines from the carved mahogany splat of this armchair of 1770–80 (detail of chair opposite), attributed to Thomas Affleck of Philadelphia

That minority of early American immigrants who came from Scandinavia or central Europe must have longed for the efficient ceramic heating stoves of their homeland. As settlers where the dominant culture was British, most Americans perpetuated the old country's use of inefficient fireplace heating, and endured the wretched service of fireplaces far longer than necessary. In Pennsylvania the Germans sensibly were not buying that variety of masochism, and by the first quarter of the eighteenth century they demanded iron stoves from local founders, who were usually English.

The resulting "five-plate" or "jamb" stoves, European in concept, were not necessarily well suited for rustic colonial America, but they worked. A closed iron firebox, set into a wall containing a chimney, was tended from a fireplace on the other side. The plan was reminiscent of grand European homes and palaces, where graceful corner stoves were stoked from hidden service rooms. The German farmers of Pennsylvania ordered their iron stoves cast with pious mottos. By 1765, the basic impracticality of the five-plate stove was too clear for it to continue, and new free-standing models appeared, connecting to the chimney through sheet-metal stovepipes. The museum has a handsome example from the foundry of Thomas Maybury, Hereford Furnace in Berks County, Pennsylvania. The device's operation would be instantly clear to any member of the modern back-to-wood-stoves movement; moreover, the handsomely proportioned rectangular appliance contains the useful refinement of a bake oven. Like a number of rare artifacts in the museum, the Maybury stove begat its own codicil to history: in 1893, at the Chicago Exposition, it attracted wide interest as America's oldest stove.

Benjamin Franklin tried his hand at inventing a stove, around 1742. His idea was good—an iron fireplace insert through which a system of air passages would save heat yet still provide the pleasure and utility of an open fire—but in practice it quickly clogged itself with soot. Stove founders began working, with some success, to improve on Franklin's design.

For Americans of the seventeenth and eighteenth centuries, life's rigors were succored by the comforts of tradition. Settlers in Virginia and Massachusetts began by trying to transplant Old World domestic surroundings but yielded in time to practical variations. One dream of what they left behind is embodied in Greenfield Village's Cotswold Cottage, a Gloucestershire house and outbuildings dating from the early seventeenth century in England. Its massive stone construction would not have been duplicated in the early colonies, yet its sturdy oak cupboards, chairs, and tables of Tudor and Jacobean styles were both imported and copied here.

A better view of the early seventeenth-century New England home comes at the village's Plympton House, originally in South Sudbury, Massachusetts. Constructed around a massive central chimney, the one-room, twenty-five-by-twenty-foot house with an upstairs loft sheltered Thomas and Abigail Plympton and their seven children. The setting of their life is

Opposite. Mary Ball Washington, mother of the first president, once owned this William and Mary high chest of drawers. It is attributed to New England, dating from very early in the 1700s

Above. This walnut high chest of drawers of the Chippendale era, a type usually known as the Philadelphia highboy, was made between 1760 and 1780

45

one we strive to duplicate today in dens and family rooms from Bridgeport to Pasadena; it would not be so rich in charm if we were required to live as the Plymptons did, cooking above the coals in rough iron utensils, spinning flax and wool, weaving fabrics, rendering lard, boiling laundry, dipping candles. Such necessities of the hearthside, plus the punishing outdoor farm work, were aspects of a self-sufficient, traditional, preindustrial society that changed little across the generations. Superficially, the eighteenth century may seem a bit more polished in such Greenfield Village manifestations as the Connecticut Saltbox House and the New Hampshire Secretary Pearson House, both from around 1750. Yet the processes of life were the same.

Fireplace cooking was uncomfortable in hot weather but demonstrably more efficient than fireplace heating. The slow change to heating by stove—picking up speed at the end of the eighteenth century in the Middle Atlantic states if not New England—was not accompanied by a similar move to *cooking* by stove. Yet at least one American started giving serious thought to shifting food from the hearth to a more reliable heat source. Benjamin Thompson was a Massachusetts-born Tory whose checkered and often distinguished career included high British government service during the American Revolution, major experiments with gunpowder, and becoming a German count, whereupon he chose the title "von Rumford" after his wife's New Hampshire birthplace. In England, near the close of the eighteenth century, Rumford made original scientific studies into the nature of heat and capped his work with radical new designs for cookstoves and roasting ovens. Rumford's principles, which concentrated and enclosed heat, were appropriated by American stovemakers and led to real breakthroughs in cooking techniques. "Rumford roasters" became the rage in progressive kitchens. The museum displays a Boston-made specimen of this handsome, cylindrical device of skillfully worked iron and brass.

Progress toward adequate lighting in the seventeenth and eighteenth centuries was, if anything, even slower than the quest for heat. The artificial light of our first colonists flickered feebly from candles, rush lights, and grease lamps. Some even used "light wood"—slivers of resin-rich pine. Candles were expensive to buy or trouble to make, yet they were preferable to the alternatives. Gradually, the smoky, smelly, rodent-attracting grease lamp was improved by inventive blacksmiths, tinsmiths, and potters. Betty lamps, spout lamps, peg lamps, Argand lamps, Phoebe lamps, pan lamps, lard lamps, pig lamps: such are some of the forgotten light makers of our earlier years that are now displayed, rank on rank, in the museum.

Even the redoubtable Count Rumford experimented with lighting, as well as with stoves and explosives, a not altogether irrelevant grouping. Fire was such a pervasive danger that in many regions of America, the kitchen was built under a separate roof in the backyard, so that when and if it caught fire the damage would be restricted. Fireplaces and open-flame

Opposite. "Living History" at the Saltbox House, performed by costumed Greenfield Village staff members, takes the visitor back to domestic scenes of rural Connecticut in the mid-1700s

Above. The Plympton House of 1638 is Greenfield Village's oldest American home. The one-room Puritan cottage came from South Sudbury, Massachusetts

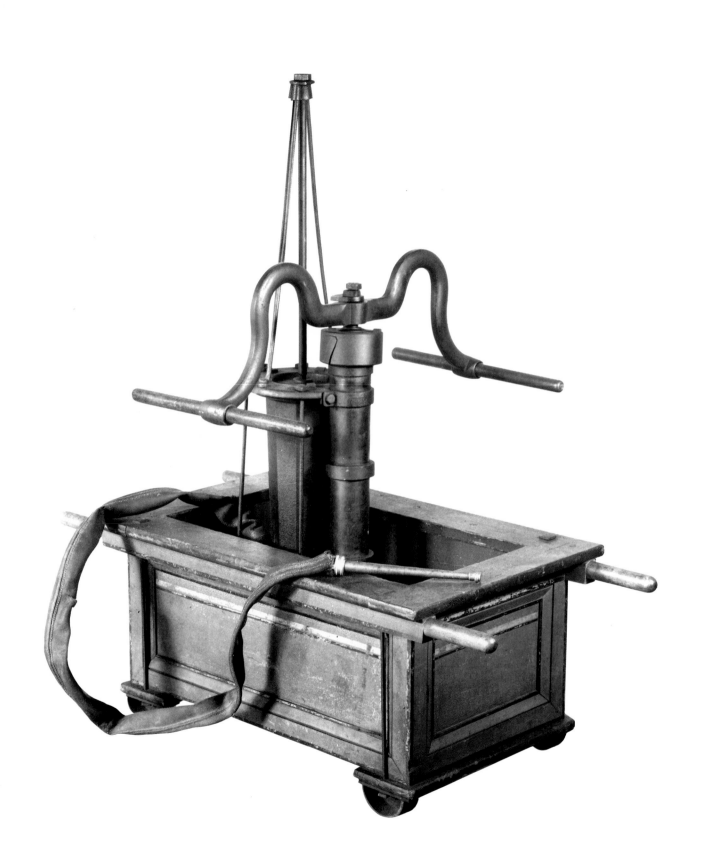

lamps took their toll in other structures as well. One of the best-selling products of colonial leatherworkers was the pitch-daubed fire bucket that hung in every hall.

Dutch inventors around 1700 produced the first fire hose for playing water forth onto a fire. By the eighteenth century, London became the European center of fire equipment manufacturing, and its best-known maker was Richard Newsham. The museum's earliest pumper is probably a Newsham, and may date from the 1760s, when it was used in New England. By the late 1700s, fire engines were made in the American colonies. Technological progress was slow, and frequently the dating of such antiques is difficult. But in restoring one early New England machine, the inscribed date 1797 handily appeared, and other clues pointed to the Boston shop of Ephraim Thayer as its manufacturer. In such establishments, the pool of mechanical skill began to grow faster.

*P*otters and glassblowers could work almost anywhere, and they quickly set up shop in America's earliest colonies. Yet the archeological record is clear that our colonial ancestors relied overwhelmingly on imports for tableware. English earthenwares arrived in America in prodigious quantities. Dutch and German pottery is also found in the trash heaps of the seventeenth and eighteenth centuries. Chinese porcelains actually made their North American debut in the 1500s, via Spanish landings on the West Coast.

Chinese wares were coveted because of the superiority of hard-paste porcelain in both service and beauty, and for the oriental refinement of ornamentation. The Chinese were quick to accommodate western taste in designs, and by 1725 the colonies were importers of porcelain through British traders. Direct trade between New York and Canton began after the Revolution with the sailing of the *Empress of China* on February 22, 1784.

The museum's vast ceramics collection includes such select specimens of the era as one piece from a set of Ching-teh-chen tea service with an unusually well-documented history, naming the Massachusetts matron for whom the set was made, and even the ship that delivered it. The prideful monogram and the classical painted scenes of goddesses and cupids suggest the upward-bound cultural strivings of New England's merchants.

The pedigree of another Chinese piece is still more distinguished. George Washington is represented by a plate of about 1785, decorated with the iconography of the newly formed Society of the Cincinnati. The plate descended in the Custis family of Virginia to Mrs. Robert E. Lee. Still another Chinese plate of between 1758 and 1783 recalls the unsuccessful social striving of William Alexander of New York, who claimed the extinct title of the Earldom of Stirling, and ordered its handsome arms emblazoned on his china.

Opposite. This small, hand-carried fire pump is the museum's oldest, and may have been made by Richard Newsham, a pioneer English manufacturer of fire equipment, in about 1760. It once served in Dudley, Massachusetts

Top. This ten-plate stove was cast in 1767 at Hereford Furnace, Berks County, Pennsylvania; it was displayed in 1893 at the Chicago Exposition, attracting the interest of antiquarians

Bottom. The well-crafted "Rumford Roaster" was made by Joseph Howe of Boston in about 1825. It was based on the 1796 invention of Sir Benjamin Thompson, an American loyalist who became Count Rumford

The potters of England were not prone to abandon the game to the Chinese, and offered a staggering variety of competitive delftware, redware, creamware, and salt-glazed stoneware, some done to the American taste. An early example is the museum's c. 1704 tin-glazed delftware plate, probably from London's Lambeth area. With its bold monogram and polychrome crown, the plate has a perky, earthy quality of intense vigor. A delftware drug jar, dated 1723 and marked P:TARTAR, originated in Bristol. An Irish-made plate of 1750 features a baroque scalloped border and, competitively, an oriental landscape in the center, all painted in blue on the tin glaze.

Delftware was superseded in popularity by other bodies, chiefly refined salt-glazed stoneware and the colorful early creamware pottery popularized by Thomas Whieldon. In the second half of the eighteenth century, the development of transfer-printed creamware and pearlware resulted in fabulous new export opportunities for the potters of Staffordshire. Ransacking American publications for patriotically commercial images, potters created such gems as the museum's 1800 pitcher from Liverpool's Herculaneum Pottery, bearing a black transfer print of George Washington clearly taken from another print, which in turn had followed a famous Gilbert Stuart portrait.

Awards and commemorations meant profitable business. An elaborate example of a private citizen's recognition is found in the museum's pitcher by Staffordshire's Wood and Caldwell Pottery. On one side, working amid the tools and products of his trade, a cooper is pictured. Beneath the spout is the legend WINE/BENJAMIN EMMONS/BORN IN BOSTON/May the 10th/1762. Cartoons, maps, naval victories, eulogies, Indian maidens, political songs, the glorious completion of canals and railroads: such were the themes, often executed with great artistry, adorning the transfer-printed English ceramics destined for America, a truly international expression of the early Industrial Revolution.

The museum's renowned glass collection is virtually all American, but begins with some English bottles of the seventeenth century. The industry's slow eighteenth-century development is traced by the work of such legendary figures as Henry W. Stiegel of Mannheim, Pennsylvania. A Stiegel pocket flask of about 1770 is only four and one-half inches tall, but is a landmark in American glass. Also rare and important is a similar, slightly larger, slightly later (c. 1785–90) bottle from the New Bremen Glass Manufactory of Maryland.

Part sculptor, part metallurgist, part salesman, the colonial silversmith created tangible expressions of his clients' wealth. Silver was not for everyone; the masses made do with pewter, wooden, or earthenware vessels and utensils. But by the end of the seventeenth century, prospering Massachusetts supported America's first galaxy of first-rate silversmiths. One was John Noyes of Boston, whose work is represented in a lovely tankard, like a sloping ring-molded cylinder with a molded flat cover. Still rarer is a rather

Opposite. This hard-paste porcelain Chinese export plate of c. 1785 was decorated in Canton with the emblem of the Society of the Cincinnati. Its associations with the Washington, Custis, and Lee families of Virginia add to its historical interest

Top. Masters of transfer printing, English potters cashed in on such commemoratory American themes as the opening of the Erie Canal

Bottom. These three pieces of Chinese porcelain, made for Massachusetts matron Abigail Goodwin, arrived in Salem on Elias Hasket Derby's ship, the *Grand Turk*

modest-looking bowl, only six inches in diameter, that the museum believes to be America's earliest intact racing trophy. Made by Jesse Kip of New York, the Kip Cup was presented to Jacob and Maria Van Dorn when their colt won a one-mile race at Middletown, New Jersey, in 1699. In this pleasant little repoussé drinking bowl, with its caryatid handles and fleurs-de-lis all slightly reminiscent of the era's William and Mary furniture designs, we discern not the first herald of the gaudy trophies of the future.

The museum's silver collection includes a c. 1770 coffeepot by Paul Revere, an excellent Rococo example with all the right details: pear-shaped body, double-domed lid, acorn finial. Revere was a multitalented figure whose primary craft—silversmithing—spanned all the best stylistic eras. Around 1785 he made an extremely rare drum-shaped teapot; by 1790 he was fully into the Federal theme with a classically straight-sided oval teapot.

In silversmithing, as in all crafts, a high standard of acquired competence was the orthodox requisite, but some craftsmen simply were gifted with greater design talent than others. Joseph Lownes of Philadelphia had talent in lavish measure: a silver tankard he made c. 1790 is a dazzling work with bold bands of horizontal grooves around a tapered cylinder, and an engraving of the brig *Lavinia.* The ship's insurance underwriters presented the tankard to the captain, clearly a man of probity and profits. And, perhaps, of luck.

Something in the deepest character of timepieces must have struggled to resist the Industrial Revolution. Horology succeeded in remaining at least partially aloof while passing through the era like everything else. One difference was that watches and clocks had been mechanical successes for centuries, long before the Industrial Revolution began. Few other devices, with the exception of the pipe organ, could make that statement. When Renaissance kings craved mechanical miracles, they were essentially limited to what the best clock and organ makers could cook up. Such craftsmen possessed a high degree of mechanical sophistication and artistry. A watchmaker of about the time that Thomas Newcomen's first crude steam engine clanked and shuddered to life might not have been terribly impressed by the invention; why, hadn't his lot for generations been making reliable machines, drawing on the predictable power source of a coiled spring?

The museum displays a watch of just that time. George Graham of London, early in the eighteenth century, fashioned this marvelous open-face example, its silver dial a mass of scallops, brass studs, and Arabic and Roman numerals. In style it echoes the seventeenth century more than it accepts the eighteenth. But throughout any era, watchmakers expressed idiosyncrasies of style. Their miniature, confined purlieu demanded personalized artistry. Appreciation of the museum's hundreds of antique watches, twinkling silently in their gallery cases, demands equally concentrated attention.

The earliest clocks to reach America were brass-cased, wall-mounted

lantern clocks, whose weights and pendulums hung in the open air. The type would soon vanish, displaced by American tall-case clocks, spring-driven bracket clocks, and various other styles. Among the best are a 1765 Pennsylvania Chippendale clock with a masterfully-carved mahogany case graced by rosettes and flame finials; a Hepplewhite clock of c. 1810 by Jacob Eby of Manheim, Pennsylvania, justly noted for its all-American curly maple case with marquetry eagle medallions; and a strikingly beautiful, complex bracket clock of 1795 by Andrew Billings of Poughkeepsie, New York. Several examples display the legendary skills of Simon and Aaron Willard of Roxbury, Massachusetts. Toward the end of his distinguished career, Thomas Harland of Norwich, Connecticut, made a lovely Federal clock of mahogany, inlaid with maple and ebony in perfect harmony. Harland, one of America's masters of the old eighteenth-century school, had an apprentice whose name would soon be even better known: Eli Terry.

Like most serious artisans, Harland executed perfectly the design orders of his time, as dictated by the Messrs. Chippendale, Hepplewhite, and Sheraton. Other Americans liked to improvise. That could work well if the craftsman commanded a sense of line and proportion. One such was the regrettably anonymous maker of a "possibly Delaware" clock. Splendid marquetry of satinwood covers the mahogany case, and the hood frieze is spangled with inlaid stars. Here, indeed, is a Hepplewhite-based clock made by a daring, exuberant, sure hand.

One of James Watt's engines was installed in a Manchester, England, cotton mill in 1785. English water power was clearly inadequate to meet the growing demand for energy. Within fifteen years, by the end of the century, Manchester would have thirty steam engines running its cotton mills. We Americans had more promising water power, but otherwise the cotton mills of New England resembled their English models, as translated by Slater's installation at Pawtucket. The year 1785 was also the year of another portentous development in textiles: the first use of roller, or cylinder, printing developed simultaneously in England and France. Eli Whitney's gin would soon multiply the supply of cheap cotton. By the mid-1800s, throughout the West, the business of making cotton cloth—calico—was thoroughly industrialized, taking the first giant step toward modern factory production.

As early as 1830, the United States counted some eight hundred cotton mills. Good printed cotton kept dropping in price and rising in quality in a consumer's bonanza that lasted for the better part of a century. A good example of the early period in the museum's collection of fabric is a long piece of unused cotton dating c. 1795. Its complex, three-color wood-block printed design is composed of blossoms, branches, and curling ribbons, an attractive and bright, polished design.

The 1700s ended in sartorial glory, at least for the wealthy, as indicated in the museum's 1780 European frock court suit, refulgent in its embroidery. Women's fashions ranged from the dainty to the dramatic, as seen by

Opposite. Brothers Simon and Aaron Willard of Massachusetts rank high in America's skilled fraternity of early-nineteenth-century clockmakers. Simon made the eight-day banjo clock at left in about 1815. In Manheim, Pennsylvania, in about 1810, Jacob Eby crafted the eagle-inlaid curly-maple tall-case clock. At right, nicely reflecting Empire tastes, is a lyre clock, c. 1825, made by Sawin & Dyer of Boston

an authentic red cold-weather hood, or cloak. But the new Republic demanded more democratic haberdashery. Even the great and popular Jefferson soon greeted White House guests in drab, worn clothes and carpet slippers.

Any study of the museum's parade of antique fashions elicits alternating sensations: surprised recognition at the familiarity of one thing, and puzzlement at the alien nature of another. One of the latter is mourning jewelry. A gold ring with a black enamel band memorializes the departure of Stephen Van Rensselaer in 1769. A ring remembering the late Elizabeth Ropes is mounted with an artificial jewel in the shape of a coffin, complete with skeleton. On mourning pins, bereaved husbands, children, and mothers slump across the tombs of their beloved. Some of the museum's memorial pins and lockets incorporate human hair.

Opposite. If an American colonist owned a watch, chances were it was English. George Graham of London made this handsome, silver-cased, open-face pocket watch in about 1740. Its silver dial has Roman and Arabic numerals; the hands are of pierced brass. Repair papers, such as the one tucked inside the case, give clues to a timepiece's later travels

Above. Honoring departed loved ones by special mourning jewelry was an accepted practice in early America; this gold locket recalls the memory of a young man of twenty-four who died in 1795

*t*he eighteenth-century American of any class was more inclined to play a musical instrument than is his modern counterpart. Violins, guitars, recorders, flutes, harpsichords, drums, jews harps: such were the popular sources of music two hundred years ago. We had to make the music if we wanted to enjoy it, in most cases, as professional musicians were scarce. The results could be elaborate, as when Thomas Jefferson led regular musicales at Monticello. Auditors were rarely surprised at the quality of those performances, for high competence was expected. At a lesser range on the social scale, there is ample testimony that if the quality of fiddling in taverns was not always so fine, at least it was lively.

The violin was the eighteenth century's lead instrument in all respects, with expressive tone, tractable volume, and universal familiarity. Even at the start of the 1700s it already had reached a stage of development that even today is deemed an apogee. That golden age is well represented in the museum's collection of musical instruments. Oldest is a spectacularly rare example from 1647 by Nicolo Amati, one of the masters of the Cremona, Italy, school of violinmaking. He was the teacher of Antonio Stradivari, who is represented by two violins, dated 1703 and 1709, in the collection. A third Olympian name represented is Joseph Guarnerius, with an instrument named The Doyen from 1741. More violins from the same era round out a supernal collection of early strings.

Few Americans would have had such instruments, yet the odds were that even the common violin was European-made. The same could be said for clarinets, oboes, viola da gambas, and guitars. The pear-shaped English guitar, favorite of eighteenth-century lady instrumentalists, was a form of medieval cittern, whose iron strings, tuned in an open chord, sounded clear but melancholy. Meanwhile the modern guitar evolved, a bit smaller than today's, and often distinguished by a bowed-out back formed of slender staves, like a barrel. Because of that back, the guitar was hard to make, but

Charles Taws, a Scottish immigrant, made beautiful pianos in Philadelphia. One of them was this lovely edition of 1794, with an inlaid Hepplewhite mahogany case and a 61-note English action

spoke with a wonderfully mellow voice. The harpsichord was another popular if expensive import. The shops in which most were made approached factory size and specialization, such as Jacob Kirckman's of London. Another great harpsichord maker of the time was London's Thomas Hitchcock, whose work is represented by the museum's 1733 specimen, one of only about twenty surviving today. Orchestral music of the eighteenth century had a much softer, mellower tone than today's counterpart. Brilliant brasses would arrive in the nineteenth century.

Some musical-instrument makers moved to the population centers of eighteenth-century America. Charles Taws, a Scottish piano maker, arrived in New York in 1786 and moved to Philadelphia in 1788 for a long and successful career. In 1794, Taws made the small square piano that is one of the museum's rarest artifacts. Its sixty-one-note keyboard, of English manufacture, is contained in a splendid Hepplewhite case of mahogany with satinwood panels. Floral flourishes, both painted and inlaid, confirm the skill of Mr. Taws's shop. That the piano was used, and not just admired, is attested by the number of repaired ivories.

The first firearms to reach the New World were clumsy, heavy, and unreliable. Most were probably matchlocks, an ancient firing device that plunged a smoldering "match" (more properly, a fuse) into the weapon's priming pan. The matchlock worked reasonably well unless one's match became damp, whereupon the weapon would not fire at all. Early militiamen were armed with such pieces. The first settlers also brought a few wheellocks, which were far more expensive and inclined to be used by the gentry for sporting purposes. The wheellock worked like a giant cigarette lighter, with a serrated wheel which, upon being cranked into readiness, would spin sparks into the priming pan. Both wheellock and matchlock were voices of the Middle Ages; another type, which a few of our early seventeenth-century ancestors carried off the boat at St. Augustine, Jamestown, and Plymouth, was the snaphance. Also called the doglock, the snaphance was an early form of flintlock that already had the basic features of the system. On triggering, the "cock" (or hammer) smacked a piece of flint carried in its jaws into a steel "frizzen," or "battery," to create a shower of sparks. By the middle of the seventeenth century, the flint system was standard almost everywhere.

Around the middle of the eighteenth century, American gunsmiths introduced a new weapon of almost magical accuracy, based on German hunting rifles brought to Pennsylvania and Virginia early in the eighteenth century. The beautiful rifle that would help tame the trans-Appalachian frontier, and make life miserable for the Redcoats, has been variously called the Kentucky rifle, Pennsylvania rifle, American long rifle, or just long rifle. The best term is American rifle, as it was made across a wide geographic range and reflected a variety of local styles, or schools. The museum's collection contains many examples of this American classic in its various

Most violins used in early America were imported, yet rare in any age or country is an instrument of this quality. It was made in Cremona, Italy, in 1647 by Nicolo Amati, who trained Antonio Stradivari and who was the most important member of a famed instrument-making family

phases, beginning with the import that served as prototype. The German Jaeger (or hunter) rifle dates from around 1750, the year usually assigned to the first American rifles. With its full walnut stock, octagonal barrel, sliding wood patch box, hickory ramrod, and engraved flintlock, there is some indication of parenthood. Yet in building their great new gun, the American makers borrowed from other styles as well.

With such sporting guns, as with coaches, clothing, furniture, and tableware, people tended to take care of the expensively made items, use them less, and then treasure them as heirlooms when they became obsolete. Therefore the homely, handy tools made for hard use, such as an American-made fowling piece of 1758, rarely survived to fall into the hands of collectors or museums. The flintlock fowler (today it would be called a shotgun) is unusual for other reasons, as well. Eighteenth-century American gunsmiths were reticent about signing and dating their work. But in this case, maker Medad Hills signed the piece, added the date and his address of Goshen, Connecticut, and inscribed the name of the customer, Noah North. Rare is the antique that carries its own pedigree so completely.

One gunsmith not only participated in America's Industrial Revolution, he helped start it. Eli Whitney has hardly been forgotten by history, but he scarcely ever gets sufficient credit for both of his mighty contributions that changed the western world. In 1793, as the guest on a Georgia plantation just after his graduation from Yale, young Whitney invented the cotton gin. The ability to mechanically separate seeds from cotton fiber proved a mixed blessing. While it resulted in cheap, abundant cotton for the world's fabric mills, it also created an irresistible demand for cheap field hands—in a word, slaves. The institution of slavery grew like an incubus in the wake of the cotton gin.

Whitney had difficulty protecting his patent for the cotton gin, and in 1798 he built a new factory at New Haven, Connecticut, to manufacture military muskets for the U.S. government. This was the setting for his second great contribution. Prior to Whitney's plunge into musket manufacturing, gunmaking had been a bench craft where each weapon was made individually of component parts formed and fitted for it alone. Whitney's master stroke was to make gun parts of such precision that the parts were interchangeable with minor fitting in assembly. The principle may seem obvious today, but it was a fundamental change in the way manufacturers looked at things.

AN
AMERICAN DICTIONARY
OF THE
ENGLISH LANGUAGE;
FIRST EDITION IN OCTAVO,
CONTAINING
THE WHOLE VOCABULARY OF THE QUARTO, WITH CORRECTIONS, IMPROVEMENTS,
AND SEVERAL THOUSAND ADDITIONAL WORDS.
TO WHICH IS PREFIXED
AN INTRODUCTORY DISSERTATION
ON THE
ORIGIN, HISTORY & CONNECTION OF THE LANGUAGES OF WESTERN ASIA & EUROPE,
WITH AN EXPLANATION
OF THE PRINCIPLES ON WHICH LANGUAGES ARE FORMED.

BY NOAH WEBSTER, LL. D.

IN TWO VOLUMES,
VOL. I.

SPRINGFIELD, MASS.

The Age of Noah Webster

*h*is name is synonymous with one of the indispensable tools of scholarship, but Noah Webster became a curiously neglected figure in American history as his personal fame somehow slipped away. He deserves a refurbished reputation. Descendant of colonial governors, combat veteran of the American Revolution, lawyer, educator, editor, politician, legislator, professor, administrator, linguist, loving father, and family man, Webster would have been a remarkable national treasure even had he not been the most prodigious lexicographer and philologist in the history of America.

His comfortable home, standing in Federal serenity in Greenfield Village, seems to reflect the man. Although he was already sixty-five when he and his wife, Rebecca, moved to their new house (then in New Haven, Connecticut), he would spend another two decades working there, and complete in 1828—in his upstairs study—the most important work of his life, *An American Dictionary of the English Language*. The project was the most ambitious of Webster's distinguished life, and it took twenty years. When the two-volume, seventy-thousand-word dictionary reached market, it became one of the great landmarks of erudition, helping impose authority on American word usage, as well as indexing thousands of words never seen in dictionaries before. Yet long before his great dictionary appeared, Webster had made a vast contribution toward the standardization of American spelling and pronunciation. His three-part *Grammatical Institute of the*

Opposite. In this upstairs study of his home in New Haven, Connecticut, Noah Webster in 1828 completed his great work, *An American Dictionary of the English Language*. Henry Ford saved the home from demolition, and reconstructed it in Greenfield Village in the 1930s. Much of the study furniture, including the desk-bookcase, is original to the house

He was no polished master from sophisticated Philadelphia, Baltimore, or Newport, but Godfrey Wilkin may be said to represent a body of capable American artisans who made furniture for the average citizen. Clearly, this mountain craftsman had a sense of humor

English Language, appearing first in 1783–85, had a profound influence on American culture. The first book, the *Blue-backed Speller,* sold more than 100 million copies over more than a century of use, gradually being replaced by *McGuffey Readers.*

Copies of Webster's historic publications rest on a work table and desk in the upstairs study of his home. The 1790 Hepplewhite desk-bookcase is the very one where he did much of his work, and the room is where he died in 1843, his amazing fount of scholarship stilled at eighty-four years.

Unlike Noah Webster, who was a scion of New England's old patrician culture, William Holmes McGuffey was born in a one-room log cabin in western Pennsylvania. The rustic little structure, built in about 1780, stands today in Greenfield Village and is furnished in the rough-hewn charm of the early nineteenth century, much as it probably looked around the time young McGuffey arrived in 1800. Despite their frontier surroundings, the McGuffeys were ambitious and intelligent, and William received a good education. He became a professional educator in Ohio, helped organize that state's public school system, and went on to a long career as professor of moral philosophy at the University of Virginia. But his incalculable influence on the mind of nineteenth-century America was based on his series of six textbooks first published in 1836, the *McGuffey Eclectic Readers.* With one reader for each elementary grade, McGuffey's illustrated books conveyed solid literary instruction in stories of common sense, patriotism, and morality based on upbeat pragmatism, not doctrinaire theology. The books dominated American education for generations, and helped mold the minds of young Henry Ford, the Wright brothers, and most of their contemporaries. Ford's high regard for McGuffey led the great mogul of Dearborn into gathering a complete set of *Readers,* which led to Ford's broader passion for collecting the entire mosaic of American life.

Around the year of McGuffey's birth, 1800, the Federal era of design was at its peak. In Salem, Massachusetts, a furniture maker named Samuel McIntyre summed up the Federal theme perfectly in a handsome Hepplewhite sideboard with skillfully carved grapes, leaves, baskets, and rosettes. The museum also has a Recamier Grecian sofa attributed to Duncan Phyfe, made between 1810 and 1820 in New York. The full force of America's revived flirtation with French design is clear in a c. 1815 card table. Probably made by the gifted Charles Honoré Lannuier, it is a stirring spectacle of gilded eagles, rosettes, and animal-paw feet. With such extravagant skill, the Empire style was ushered in by trend-setting New York masters, who had no way of knowing that their final orders would lead straight to those Empire adaptations seized upon (and, critics say, sadly degraded) by pioneering factories in the antebellum age.

Not all the Federal era's output was of such bon ton. That time of self-confident expansion demanded sturdy furniture of all kinds, and many unsung cabinetmakers, often working in walnut, created a body of early

nineteenth-century furniture from which collectors still choose many desirable pieces. Any fancier of Americana would be delighted to find a duplicate of the museum's blanket chest from mountainous Hardy County, Virginia, made by Godfrey Wilkin, a man of obviously irrepressible drollery. The front of this big, complex walnut and pine chest bears the self-congratulating legend "WEL DON" (twice) and then the vertical commands "READ THES UP" and "AND READ THES DOWN." We even know the first owner: "JACOB WILKIN HIS CHEAST." Jacob *must* have been pleased.

The new century's rapid improvement in foundry technology began paving the way for a dramatic upgrading in household hardware. First came a proliferation of variants on the original Franklin stove. Despite the design's original drawbacks, the combined Franklin name and fireplace-stove idea enjoyed wide appeal (as it does, indeed, in our own time) and was essayed endlessly by various founders. The museum displays an 1816 Franklin by James Wilson of Poughkeepsie, New York, who was first to patent under the Franklin name. A Federal design with an eagle, stars, urn-shaped brass finials and pierced brass fender, the Franklin sprouts a towering conical heat chamber, shaped like a wizard's cap, whose function was to trap and radiate heat in the lucky owner's parlor. Its efficiency was doubtful, but it was a resplendent creation for the hearth, and something to brag about. It was clear proof of a manufacturer's willingness to experiment, and a customer's inclination to try anything once.

Foundryman Wilson's refulgent Franklin was not the stove of destiny. Vastly improved free-standing box stoves, descendants of the eighteenth-century six-plate stoves beloved of German immigrants, warmed the chambers of America during the administrations of John Quincy Adams and Andrew Jackson.

New York State became the center of the stove industry; Troy alone counted some two hundred stove manufacturers prior to the Civil War. In becoming a factory center, the Hudson River city symbolized the Industrial Revolution's rapid shift from scattered, small, traditional craft shops. Moreover, Troy's iron founders had a handy new resource for technical information: Rensselaer Polytechnic Institute, founded in 1824, is America's oldest school of engineering and science.

Modern stoves are drab imitations of their nineteenth-century ancestors. Fashion demanded that parlor or heating stoves, whether coal- or wood-burning, complement the architectural and decorative themes of the day. Consider the ensemble of grapes, roses, fruits, morning glories, and little girls adorning the 1845 J. S. and M. Peckham parlor stove from Utica. Virtually every shape of the Rococo revival writhes across its black surfaces. Another of the museum's stoves, Troy-made by G. W. Eddy in 1853, sums up the Gothic revival movement in its stars, diamonds, arches, and castle crenellations. Precisely the same well-developed design themes appear elsewhere in the same era, in seemingly unrelated artifacts like the museum's

Opposite. As iron founders enhanced their skills early in the nineteenth century, there was a great urge to create more efficient home heat sources. Early efforts, such as this 1816 Franklin fireplace unit by James Wilson, struggled to attain marginal improvement over the regular fireplace

Above. By 1845, when J. S. & M. Peckham of Utica, New York, patented this elaborate parlor stove, such units worked well

toy banks and machine tools. Another antebellum Troy stove, patented in 1853 by J. C. Fletcher, features a huge round wreath above the firebox and encircling the flue, all supported by an equally leafy, sinuously bowed base. Like many of its brethren, the stove was dished out at the top to hold a container of humidifying perfume or water. The museum's stove collection is the best in the world, and nowhere are the examples richer and more exuberant than in the wonderful parlor stoves of America's early Victorian period.

The museum's oldest full-fledged cook stove was patented in 1832 by M. N. Stanley of New York City. Stanley's ingenious creation grafted a large rotating top with four lids onto a firebox, and vented itself through two ver-

tical columns at the rear, which supported and heated a cylindrical oven. Odd as the stove may seem, it heralded the clear outline of all future cook stoves, whose shapes would last nearly a century and persist into the era of gas and electricity.

Acceptance of the cook stove was gradual, and as late as the 1840s the average American still cooked on the hearth. But the first half of the 1800s ended with a rapid shift to newly improved stoves. Meanwhile, other changes presaged a new era in the kitchen. Light, efficient tinware—often brightly painted—began replacing heavier, more expensive iron pots and pans early in the century. By 1825, helpful and popular books on cooking and home management appeared with increasing frequency. One of the best was written by an aristocratic Virginia matron, Mrs. Mary Randolph, whose *The Virginia Housewife, or, Methodical Cook* appeared in 1824. It was a national best-seller for more than seventy-five years; in her second edition of 1825 she presented her own excellent design for a refrigerator. The home was definitely attracting attention.

Aesthetics played a large role in the acceptance of another ubiquitous household device, the sewing machine, which, contrary to folklore, was not invented by Isaac Singer. Like many comparable devices, its origins (in the eighteenth century) are obscure, and its development was by committee. American Elias Howe made an important contribution around 1840 when he built a pioneering machine that provided a basis for things to come. Competition was intense by the 1850s. Sewing machines, and the strategy to sell them, provided one of the first major battlegrounds of capitalist consumerism. Curiously, there was some formidable initial resistance to the machine for reasons beyond its necessarily stiff price. The Victorian cult of domesticity, wherein woman's function was more precisely defined than at any other point in Western history, was approaching its apogee of elaborate refinement. A machine in the home would certainly alter one of woman's most ancient roles—slave to the needle—but in what way? Would it affect her femininity or corrupt her moral superiority to men? Ducking volleys of moralistic gibberish on such subjects, manufacturers cleverly advertised that sewing machine users would benefit their health via lessened drudgery, and that they would gain leisure time for rest and refinement and for setting uplifting examples for their children. It was a potent and effective appeal.

Innovations in weaving wool fabrics came soon after the first floods of cheap, printed cotton calico. In 1804, French innovator J. M. Jacquard perfected an attachment for power looms that automatically guided the repetition of a given pattern. Such a technique did not immediately displace the ancient home tradition of carding, spinning, dying, and weaving, but by the end of the first half of the nineteenth century such activities had generally disappeared. Later, in the fabric-short Confederate states, women dusted off their grandmothers' spinning wheels and looms with a resigned sense of pioneering. The museum's collection of antebellum fabrics covers

the full range of styles and techniques. One familiar American coverlet pattern dating around 1820 is a mosaic weave of blue wool and natural cotton, the once-familiar "summer-winter" pattern. About two decades later, a professional weaver created the museum's handsome Jacquard coverlet of red and indigo wool, with a quatrefoil medallion alternating with a diamond, each containing flowers. The technique of roller printing on cotton, as well as women's fashion, is illustrated in a striking dress of navy blue, yellow, and gold print.

Quilting, sometimes perceived as one of the last bastions of handwork today, was paradoxically stimulated by the avalanche of machine-made cotton. The museum's quilt collection is a rare treasury of Americana. One big "friendship" quilt of 1844 contains forty-nine squares bearing the names of friends and contributors. Some quilts contain one-of-a-kind designs, as in Susan McCord's 1880 masterpiece from Indiana, with its five-inch-wide strips of undulating floral displays.

In men's fashions, trousers replaced knee breeches, and boots paradoxically superseded low-cut, buckled shoes, which had been very comfortable despite their neither-left-nor-right construction. The accretion of years brought changes in cut and silhouette of coats and trousers, a century-long proliferation of hats, and a free attitude toward waistcoats, as expressed in the museum's star vest specimens: a sporting vest of red plush, another of embroidered moosehair.

Before the 1840s, when the Industrial Revolution struck the carpet industry, all American carpets were woven by hand. Ten years later, a power-driven carpet loom was producing at least thirty yards of ingrain, flat-woven carpet per day. The price, naturally, plummeted, and colorful, intricately patterned floor coverings were suddenly within the reach of many. Such carpeting came in strips that could be joined to cover space of any size, often wall-to-wall.

*t*oward the end of the eighteenth century it had become apparent that some glazed earthenware vessels were dispensing lead poisoning to their users. One type of reliable pottery with a clear safety record was stoneware, which had been manufactured in Europe since the Renaissance. German and English potters introduced salt-glazed stoneware to the colonies early in the eighteenth century, and after 1785 there was a conscious effort to encourage its use. Most production was concentrated in the Northeast, where salt-glazing was used exclusively on stoneware. Yet a curious anomaly occurred in the South, where an entirely different technique—using wood ash or other alkaline material—somehow emerged. Elsewhere, the process was found only in the Orient. It isn't known whether there was a connection or whether isolated southern potters reinvented the technique. The museum displays handsome examples of this southern style.

Opposite. American porcelain maker William Ellis Tucker of Philadelphia made this soft-paste pitcher in 1828

Above. This earthenware pitcher, c. 1836–42, came from the Salamander Works of Woodbridge, New Jersey. It was made for a hotel or tavern called Kidd's Troy House

Most stoneware, however, resembles the museum's Liberty jug made in 1807 in South Amboy, New Jersey, or the little 1805 Crolius inkwell from New York, or the big six-gallon crock of the mid-nineteenth century that has the name and address of a New York City grocer and a cobalt slip decoration of a free-form eagle in flight. ("Slip" is a combination of clay and water.) Cobalt was a favorite form of embellishment on the gray, hard ware; a little went a long way, and endured the necessarily high firing temperature. Such stoneware reached its peak of popularity about 1840, yet would be used well into the twentieth century as a standard vessel for food storage and preparation.

Moravian immigrants brought Germanic traditions of pottery to North Carolina in the middle eighteenth century. A deep-dish example from about 1800 displays a flattened rim decorated in slip with a tulip surrounded by scrolls and leaves. A nine-inch-tall tankard bears tulips and stylized feathers in green, red, and yellow slip. A Moravian pitcher is covered with a design of capricious scrolls and dots in yellow, brown, and green.

The Moravians' northern cousins, the Germans of Pennsylvania, made slip-decorated redware as well, but also employed the scratched or "sgraffito" technique in decorating. An eleven-inch pie plate dated 1818, from Bucks County, seems the very picture of Pennsylvania decoration: its maker, Andrew Headman, scratched in an assured eight-pointed star surrounded by tulips and other blossoms.

Craftsmen enjoyed writing all sorts of legends on their wares. Some were personal expressions; some were obviously by commercial request. One big redware plate, c. 1825, is slip decorated with the provocative message, "Cheap for Cash/only ⅓." Another is emblazoned, "Plum Pudding." A stoneware jug carries the legend, in a slightly tipsy hand, "Here's to Good Old Rum/Drink Her Down."

The nineteenth century delivered a rich harvest of glass bottles and flasks. Masonic emblems caparison a deep amethyst flask made in New England around 1820. A greenish-yellow, violin-shaped pint flask from Pittsburgh recalls the days of 1835. Still another pint is considered unique in color: the c. 1836 bottle from Coffin & Hay of New Jersey made of opaque white glass. Its patriotic ornaments include an eagle, stars, shield, and flag, and the motto, "FOR OUR COUNTRY." An early steam locomotive is molded into a blue flask, c. 1850, from Lancaster, New York, with the toast, "Success to the Railroad." A baffling Philadelphia-made quart bottle of 1851 displays a uniformed image of Louis Kossuth, an exiled Hungarian patriot, on one side, while the other side displays a side-wheeled steamer labeled "U.S. Steam Frigate Mississippi."

A wealth of commercial and utility jars and bottles speaks to the viewer with near-universal appeal. Some still bear ancient paper labels, such as the pepper sauce bottle of about 1850, a Gothic shape of aquamarine glass. Perhaps the contents—bottled by Boston's W. K. Lewis—were too hot for

Opposite. This group of American lead-glazed earthenware dates from 1820 to 1860. The dishes in front and at left are slip decorated; the Pennsylvania-made dish at upper right is ornamented by the sgraffito technique

human consumption, for the dried remains are still in the bottle. No such fate befell the cargo of another bottle, which cleverly reproduces a log cabin, its chimney comprising the neck, through which was decanted (around 1860) "E. G. BOOZ'S OLD CABIN WHISKEY." But most bottles of the Civil War era were more restrained, even elegant, such as the antebellum pickle bottle that richly displays the features of high Victorian Gothic.

Pittsburgh was a major center of cut and engraved glass production from about 1820 to 1850. That early talent is confirmed by a glass tumbler of 1825 with a deep cut panel and flutes, and a jewel-like sulfide bust of De Witt Clinton in the bottom and his initials engraved on the side. The glass was one of a presentation set for the popular New York politician celebrating the Erie Canal opening. An elaborately cut Pittsburgh punch bowl dates from about the same time, as does a heavy blown and cut decanter with applied rings. Pittsburgh also was in the vanguard of the first major application of mass production to the glass industry—*pressing* glass into molds. The technique enabled glassmakers to provide inexpensive, matched sets of ware for the first time, a boon to society and business alike. The clever, inventive production spirit thus released was even applied to windowpanes, like the museum's c. 1840 high Gothic five-by-seven-inch pane from Bakewell of Pittsburgh.

It was the Boston and Sandwich Glass Company of Massachusetts whose shortened name—"Sandwich" glass—came to mean almost all lacy pressed glass. Plainly, much good pressed glass was made by other manufacturers, although Sandwich tended to get the credit. The museum's wealth of authentic Sandwich-made glass includes a showy covered dish, c. 1830, with complex Gothic designs. A tiny cup plate, less than four inches in diameter, pictures the just-finished Bunker Hill monument at Boston, and gallantly adds, "Finished by the Ladies 1841." If you ever wondered why so much American Empire-period furniture has glass knobs, the Sandwich works, with many others, turned them out in quantity. A pair from about 1830 reveals the ingenuity of Sandwich's great founder, Deming Jarves.

The need for lamps meant good business for the glass industry. Pioneers like Thomas Cains, at his South Boston Flint Glass Works, turned out handsome whale-oil lamps by a combination of free-blowing with pattern molding. A technique called "pillar molding" came a bit later in the nineteenth century, and produced such museum standouts as a pair of c. 1845 green vases, more than a foot high.

With Ohio in the lead, the Midwest developed surprisingly early as a glassmaking center. An anonymous early nineteenth-century Ohioan had the skill to make a handsome, aquamarine one-gallon bottle with thirty swirled ribs.

America's first would-be porcelain makers must have envied the far greater success of the nation's potters and glassmakers. In 1770, two Philadelphians had attempted the eighteenth century's only commercial output

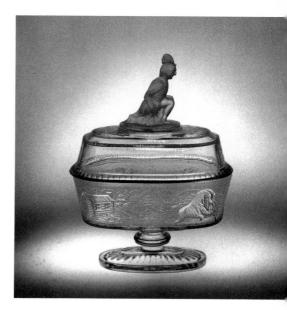

Opposite. Both these cut-glass pitchers are incised in Anglo-Irish style. The pitcher at left is attributed to England, while the smaller one probably came from Pittsburgh, Pennsylvania

Top. Three pitchers illustrate early and middle nineteenth-century American styling. The example at left, pattern-molded with twenty-four ribs, was probably made in the Midwest, 1815–35. The center pitcher, footed and loop decorated, probably was made in New Jersey, 1830–70. The larger amethyst, pillar-molded example—about two quarts in capacity—may have originated in Pittsburgh, 1840–70

Bottom. This oval covered compote of pressed pattern glass was made by Gillinder & Sons of Philadelphia, 1876–80. Originally termed "Pioneer," it is now called "Westward-Ho" by collectors

These figured flasks came from the eastern United States in 1815–55. Themes of these pint and quart containers included patriotism, politics, fraternity, and even pride in corn distribution

of porcelain, though production ended after two years. In 1826, another Philadelphian, William Ellis Tucker, mounted a major, and more successful, try at making soft-paste, bone-ash porcelain. He followed the styles of the enormously popular English and French porcelain of the day, and made such deft pieces as the museum's 1828 pitcher with a gilded lip and foot, and flowers of blue, red, and gold. The collection of Tucker's work is outstanding, presenting clear proof of his quality and skill. But despite the manifest abilities of Tucker and later American porcelain makers in the middle nineteenth century, their countrymen preferred to import from the Continent and Britain.

About 1825, on schedule with many other crafts and manufactures, silversmithing was overtaken by the Industrial Revolution. The first major change replaced the very heart of the craft, which had always been the hammering of a shape from sheet silver. The smith customarily—and noisily—"raised" hollow vessels on small anvils called "stakes." But a new technique called "spinning" used the lathe to accomplish the same end in a fraction of the time. Electroplating arrived in the 1840s. When that technique was combined with mass-produced base-metal castings and stampings, matched sets of beautiful but inexpensive tableware were possible at last. The new technique quickly drove out an earlier mechanical process—Sheffield plate—which combined silver and copper.

It also drove out pewter, hitherto indispensable as ware for the multitudes. Pewter's uses and styles paralleled those of silver, but the handy alloy was far cheaper and easier to work. Pewter followed silver through the new spinning process around 1825, and meanwhile was improved and hardened in a new generation of metallurgy called "britannia." Ironically, early electroplaters discovered that britannia was a perfect vehicle on which to plate silver, and thus pewter's final form was swallowed up in the rush for plated silver. After the 1840s, pewter virtually disappeared from the scene. The museum's collection of American and English pewter is among the world's best, affording a definitive study of such pieces as early seventeenth-century flagons to a tea set by Josiah Danforth made in about 1830.

Opposite. Two examples of nineteenth-century American stoneware display an exuberant, earthy character. The rum jug at left dates from 1865–85; the water cooler from 1835–60

Above. These two graceful pieces were made by William Ellis Tucker in about 1830. Despite such native talent, however, Americans would prefer European porcelain for many decades to come

*C*rashing chords on the piano (or pianoforte, as it was first called) heralded the future of music as the nineteenth century began. The harpsichord was already passé. Another instrument on its way to obscurity was the serpent, part woodwind and part brass, which despite its unfortunate (and altogether descriptive) name had been playing the orchestral bass part since the 1600s. The museum's oldest example of this curious instrument is an English serpent from c. 1800, made of wood, leather, and brass, with six fingerholes and three flat keys. Another English import, dating from 1840, shows the rapid sophistication of key action, as it was made with fourteen brass keys.

HALLS' QUADRILLE AND CONCERT BAND.

of the Boston Brass Band.

Woodwinds of the early nineteenth century were handsomely made and rather modern-looking; to the casual observer, the chief difference is in their construction materials, typically a mellow blonde boxwood, trimmed in ivory and brass, with brass keys. Two good museum examples are a c. 1812 oboe, made by Uzal Miner in Hartford, Connecticut, and a c. 1840 clarinet in B-flat, made by Graves & Co. with great sophistication.

The nineteenth century began with clarinets and oboes playing the musical lead, and with wind instrument technology much as it had been for more than a century. But enormous changes were coming. The keyed bugle, arriving after 1810, had a dramatic influence in at last permitting the soprano brass to play the melody. Keyed and valved brass instruments became the rage in the 1830s, and with them came the rise of all-brass bands. By 1834 came the first known trumpet battle (at Niblo's Pleasure Garden in New York), a genre that would create almost hysterical excitement. Soon America had a new class of heroes, its virtuoso brass soloists. The keyed bugle was their instrument of choice, with its larger relative the ophicleide a strong second. Handsome Edward (Ned) Kendall, who burst gloriously forth in 1835 at the head of the twenty-man Boston Brass Band, was a famous antebellum horn man. The museum, which has the world's finest collection of American brass instruments (anchored on the famous D. S. Pillsbury Collection), has the actual horns used by the Boston Brass Band in its electrifying debut, after which most bands in the country converted to all brass.

Not only were the new-style horns impressive in performance, they looked resplendent. Many were made of copper, like Ned Kendall's 1837 model by Graves & Co., but others employed brass, silver, and even solid gold. Manufacturers strove to secure the endorsements of the new class of hero-maestro, and admirers lavished the soloists with presentation instruments. Some of the finest keyed bugles were made by E. G. Wright of Boston. The museum displays several Wrights, one of them, c. 1850, made of silver with a beautifully engraved bell garland. But the ultimate is a solid gold example of 1850.

Already, by that year, the day of the key system for brass was growing short. Valve-operated horns were becoming popular. In 1856, a great battle occurred in Salem, Massachusetts, between Kendall on the keyed bugle and Patrick Gilmore on the valve cornet. It was a classic case of the young upstart, Gilmore, seeking to overturn the great veteran; the contest was judged a draw. When Kendall died in 1861, his old band played at his funeral while the master's silver bugle lay atop his coffin.

The popularity of brass bands can be explained in terms of the vast range of events where they played: circuses, dances and balls, concerts, funerals, military and firemen's musters, pleasure gardens, parades, political events, theatricals, and picnics. Star bandsmen made good incomes and traveled widely.

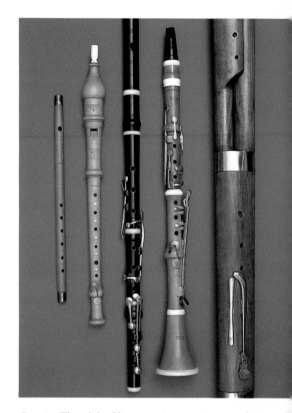

Opposite. The solid-gold presentation trumpet was made in 1866 by Hall & Quinby of Boston and presented to Rhodolph Hall (second from left) by his friends. Hall and his brother David (far left) were prominent musicians and instrument makers. (Lithograph, c. 1855, courtesy Lyme Historians, Inc., Lyme, New Hampshire)

Above. American-made woodwinds of the early nineteenth century include (from left): fife, c. 1812; flageolet, c. 1845; flute, c. 1840; clarinet, c. 1840; and bassoon, c. 1814. Until the 1840s, American bands consisted mostly of woodwinds

By the Civil War's outbreak, brass bands were armed with a multitude of sophisticated valve instruments. For a time, "overshoulder" horns were the rage, blasting their sound backward into the following marchers. The museum's musical collection is rich in many areas, but from the period around 1865 it is overpowering. We can see precisely how a band was equipped, with such instruments as a brass Isaac Fiske valve bugle, a John F. Stratton alto horn, a German silver baritone horn by J. Lathrop Allen, and a brass and German silver tuba by Moses Slater.

America's fascination with its town bands lasted throughout the nineteenth century, and well into the twentieth. Popular as they were, brass bands and their instruments did not supplant other types of music. At big dances, a brass band would alternate with a strings and reeds ensemble. But it was in helping produce music for the home that American manufacturers had their greatest opportunity. Pianos, pump organs, music boxes, dulcimers, guitars, banjos: such instruments of mechanical ingenuity were very important in the pre-electronic age. One touching artifact is a guitar once used by Stephen Foster, a spruce and rosewood instrument of the 1840s made by C. F. Martin of New York. A grand harmonicon (or set of musical glasses) further suggests the diversity of nineteenth-century music.

The reed organ and piano collection, blending furniture with the apparatus of musicianship, is the most beautiful display in the museum's large music gallery. Reed, pump, or parlor organs came in with the nineteenth century, and enjoyed more than a hundred years of popularity. By any exacting standard, their sound alternated between an asthmatic wheeze and an insipid whine. Yet they were cheaper than pianos, and not a bit harder to play, once you mastered the technique of alternately pumping the carpet-covered foot pedals. A degree of easy fun came in working the stops. Unlike pianos, reed organs could be made in almost any size, to suit rooms from meager to magnificent. There was even a rocker lap organ, a sort of semi-accordion, that went by the grand name "elbow melodeon." The instrument was rocked or pumped with the left forearm, while both hands played the button or keyboard action. The museum has both kinds; the rarest is an 1840 Bartlet from Concord, New Hampshire, with ivory button keys.

While the musical performance of any reed organ was limited, the maker could let himself go in producing a case for it at the highest level of American cabinetry. An early nineteenth-century New York-made organ by Peloubet, Pelton & Co. supports its classically plain box on lyre-styled pedestals, all of rosewood. In 1869, the Empire Organ Co. of Kalamazoo, Michigan, produced a Rococo organ to rival the skill of a London cabinet-maker in the years of George III, a cabriole-legged masterpiece of rosewood and curly maple, with a six-octave range. In the later Victorian Renaissance revival and Eastlake eras, major organs grew pompously in tiered layers festooned with fretwork and turnings, but always to high standards of cabinetry. A famous Fort Wayne Organ Co. specimen dominates the collection.

Opposite. In America, the minstrel show was an enormously popular entertainment form, beginning in the 1840s, peaking in the fifties and sixties, but enduring well into the twentieth century. Crucial to the minstrel show's success were banjo, fiddle, bones, and lively musical scores. Those elements are all present here, and American-made: violin, c. 1840; banjo, c. 1860; bones, c. 1900. Stephen Foster's *Ring De Banjo* was published in 1851

Above. This square piano in a Duncan Phyfe-style case was made by Gibson & Davis of New York City, c. 1820

Of all the instruments enjoyed by our nineteenth-century forebears, the violin, guitar, and piano have the most relevance in our time. The museum's piano collection reveals the rich variety that was available. Pianos of the late Federal–early Empire period were small, but what a wealth of skill went into the execution of such instruments as the Duncan Phyfe (works by Davis and Gibson) of 1820! Its mahogany case is accented by a pierced fallboard, and satinwood and brass inlays; pedestals are heavily carved and connected by a turned, reeded stretcher. The piano's works are framed in wood, in what was termed the "English square action" of sixty-eight notes.

Pianos grew larger with the development of full iron frames. By the 1850s, the instrument had reached the massive scale that would endure the heavy thumping of the Civil War years. An 1855 T. Gilbert & Co. piano of Boston is typical, with mighty, turned legs that would support a hippopotamus. The key total was now up to eighty-five.

Clockmaker Eli Terry and his slightly later Connecticut contemporary Seth Thomas spent the early years of the nineteenth century producing so many good, inexpensive mantel clocks that soon the grand old tall case clock was rendered almost extinct. Pillar and scroll, column and cornice, banjo, ogee: the clocks of New England's factories surged across America on waves of Yankee peddlers. One Seth Thomas column and cornice clock, with its heavy "degraded Empire" look, offers a clear view of the taste of the early Victorian middle class. Elsewhere, very few tall case clocks continued to be made, including dwarfs of approximately half size—such as the museum's 1820 example by Connecticut's Reuben Tower—which seemed to lose the grace, as well as the majesty, of the tall originals. A final raucous echo of the benchcrafted tall case era comes in a gigantic c. 1850 Soap Hollow, Pennsylvania, clock of painted pine.

In the watchmaking trade, manufacturers power stamped their moving parts by 1850, and by 1870—when knurled stems replaced the ancient keywind system—factory standardization dominated the industry. But individual craftsmen endured, particularly those who made complex chronometers and beautiful cases. In watchmaking, as in few other crafts, skill at the bench survived the Industrial Revolution relatively intact.

On the farm, change arrived on the point of an excellent new cast-iron plow. Several fledgling manufacturers produced them, but the most successful was Jethro Wood of Scipio, New York, who had the grace to credit Thomas Jefferson for his contributions to improved plow design. By 1820, eastern American farmers could till their fields with reasonable satisfaction. But the newly opening Midwest presented a new problem: although the prairie lands were flat and fertile, their rich black soil gummed up the moldboard of every plow known to man. Responding to that challenge was young blacksmith John Deere, newly moved from Vermont to Grand Detour, Illinois. In 1838, Deere created a steel-tipped, polished iron plow of beautiful

simplicity, much like a smoothly curving flat diamond, and with it farmers broke the Great Plains. The museum's example dates from Deere's early career, before he moved to Moline in 1847 and, armed with newly plentiful steel plate from Pittsburgh, became one of the giants of agricultural manufacturing.

But if better plows increased the acreage one man could till, the farming cycle's other end, harvest, remained a great bottleneck. The pattern of mechanization was such that as a new type of machine solved one problem, other innovators leaped to improve on something else. Harvesting hay and small grains with scythe and sickle demanded such timing and manpower as to control the farm's upper limit of crop acreage and animal population. Look at the museum's collection of cutting tools, hay rakes, and turning forks, and imagine the day of a field hand at harvest time. Haymaking, which was particularly onerous, received America's first substitution of horse for human power around 1800, with adoption of the drag hay rake. Soon, a pair of clever Pennsylvanians invented the revolving hay rake, called the "American flip-flop," one of the great labor-saving devices of all time. One man and a horse could now do the work of eight field hands. The museum's wooden-toothed example of this clever machine dates from about 1840.

Shifting the human harvest burden to horse and machine reached a point of high drama in the 1830s. On his farm in Virginia's Shenandoah Valley near Staunton, young Cyrus Hall McCormick demonstrated the first successful grain reaper. McCormick inherited the project from his father, who had wearily given it up after two decades of tinkering. But after his initial success, young McCormick's dilatoriness about seeking a patent allowed Obed Hussey of Baltimore to register first, in 1833. The age seethed with reaper experimenters: Enoch Ambler of New York produced his spike-wheeled contraption in 1834, and promptly mowed down one hundred acres of Montgomery County hay. That same machine, now displayed in the museum, is believed to be America's oldest surviving harvester, a relic of incalculable significance. Apparently, little financial benefit accrued to Ambler or his backers, who sold only a few machines.

By about 1850, reapers were mechanically efficient and commercially successful. McCormick, whose machine combined all the right elements of design, correctly foresaw a vaster future market on the prairies than in the rolling Shenandoah bluegrass, and moved to Chicago in 1847 to make the famous machine that solved the ancient dilemmas of harvesting.

But many others helped, and they are represented in the museum's rich collection of mid-nineteenth-century farm equipment: Champion, Empire, Kirby's, New Yorker, Peerless, and Triumph. They weighed around 1,000 pounds each, and cost about $100. Most could cut from twelve to fifteen acres of grain per day, compared to less than one by a man with a scythe. Manny's Patent Reaper of 1853 is a good example of the reliable equipment available before the Civil War. The Manny was a rugged and popular machine whose production totals, in only two years, forged past those of the industry leader. McCormick promptly sued for patent infringement. Laboring in Manny's successful defense was a prairie lawyer just commencing his second effort at a political career: ex-Congressman Abraham Lincoln.

Lawsuits were merely part of doing business in the rough-and-tumble world of mid-century manufacturing. Another major case is recalled in the collection's prized New Yorker reaper of 1852, one of the most successful early machines. That it bears a strong resemblance to McCormick's designs of the late 1840s may not have been entirely coincidental, for at that time its manufacturer, Seymour & Morgan of Brockport, New York, was licensed by McCormick to make his "Virginia Reaper." McCormick was successful in throttling the 1852 New Yorker, whereupon the company brought out a new, slightly more original model in 1853. It was a big success for almost twenty years.

*a*ndrew Jackson's riflemen shocked the British with the accuracy of American rifles at the Battle of New Orleans. Meanwhile, the frontier of the Old Northwest was vanishing. As the novels of James Fenimore Cooper began to flow, the legend of the brave, buckskin-clad rifleman raged into vogue, creating a fresh demand for long rifles. They grew fancier in ornamentation, with more inlays of brass and coin silver. Deer, horses, dogs, hex signs, Masonic emblems, hearts, acorns, stars, eagles, and initials marched across the curly maple stocks of early nineteenth-century American rifles like a parade of folk-art icons. The museum even has one gunsmith's special set of patterns for shaping such a menagerie. Many guns so garnished were clearly created for ceremony more than actual use. But at least some duly impressed British officers, after the War of 1812, bought long rifles and took them home. The American rifle might not be the equal of British weapons in fit and polish, but it was marvelously accurate and pleasant to use.

One of the handsomest in the museum is an Ohio-made rifle of about 1830 attributed to Grant Scott of Coshocton. Its .52 caliber was a bit heavier than average for its time, for as big game receded with the advance of settlement, bores tended to shrink to sizes more suitable for squirrel or varmints. The Scott rifle is also unusual in having a walnut, rather than the standard curly maple, stock. Lavishly bedizened with silver inlays, the gun is rare in flaunting also a silver buttplate, trigger guard, and patch box.

Rarer than American rifles are American pistols, and the rarest of all is a matched pair. The museum's superb brace of .44 caliber twin flintlocks made in the Bedford County style by Peter White of Uniontown, Pennsylvania, dates c. 1820. Each piece is skillfully set with fifteen engraved silver inlays.

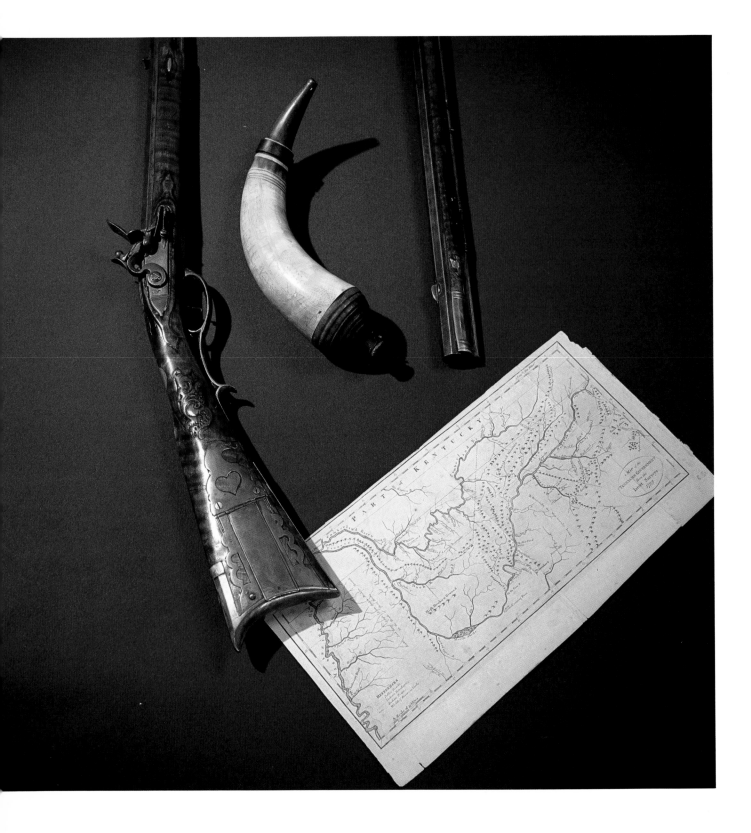

But such bench-made guns were almost things of the past. Gunmaker John Hall was already taking the final step to a modern manufacturing process, and in a sense completing the broader basis for the Industrial Revolution. Armed with a government contract, Hall in 1819 established a private factory in the shadow of the big government armory at Harpers Ferry, Virginia, and produced breechloading muskets from parts that were completely interchangeable without hand fitting, finishing the phase begun by Eli Whitney. The museum displays two Hall muskets, tangible links with a singularly innovative development.

Apart from a few significant exceptions, the museum's weapon collection is civilian, or sporting. The need to shoot faster, farther, and straighter was a preoccupation as America headed west. Gunsmiths had labored to make successful repeaters for centuries but were frustrated by crude systems of loading and ignition. After 1800, Scottish clergyman Alexander Forsythe compounded a priming substance that would explode on impact. The museum demonstrates that turning point with a rare Forsythe pistol.

After 1815, the famous percussion cap was introduced by several inventors, and that little copper detonator soon displaced the flintlock and opened the way for efficient, deadly repeaters. Among the first to manufacture was Samuel Colt of Hartford, Connecticut, who began making revolvers in Paterson, New Jersey, in 1836. The first Colts have long been the ultimate desires of gun collectors, for the flamboyant Colt went bankrupt in 1842, and "Patersons" were, and are, few. The museum displays a supernal specimen, rare even for a Paterson—an 1837 revolving rifle. With such a wonder, a rifleman could get off eight shots before reloading.

Colt recovered his fortunes with the help of the settlement of Texas and the demands of the Mexican War. He established his celebrated factory at Hartford, producing a torrent of the potent "equalizers" that, for all their stormy propensities, were also handsome examples of industrial design, and among the most successful early precision products of completely interchangeable parts. The museum shows a wide selection of models and shapes, from intimidating "Dragoon" .44s to graceful "belt" models.

Colt could not supply all the nation's demand for newfangled weaponry, and other creative gunmakers had ideas. Colt's percussion system was loaded from the cylinder's front, with paper cartridges; Smith and Wesson of Springfield, Massachusetts, outfoxed Colt by patenting cylinders bored all the way through, thus capturing for a critical time (the Civil War years) the market for revolvers that fired metallic cartridges. Such loads, invented in the 1850s, were clearly the future's ammunition, though initially they were feeble and unreliable. Another early experimenter with metal cartridges was the Volcanic Repeating Arms Co. of New Haven, Connecticut, maker of the first lever-action gun. The museum displays a Volcanic lever-action pistol of 1854. Not surprisingly, in the fast-moving early days of Yankee big industry, talent cross-pollinated. Both Horace Smith and Dan-

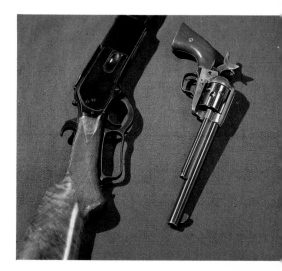

Opposite. A classic by an unknown hand, the American long rifle (left) dates from about 1820. Also unknown is the origin of the powder horn, scrimshawed with the alphabet and with leaf and animal designs. The other rifle, 1825—only its muzzle is visible—came from a Pennsylvania shop. The 1799 map evokes the old frontier, where the long rifle was indispensable

Top. Two weapons that loomed large in the American West's rambunctious final quarter were the Model 1876 Winchester rifle (left) and the 1873 Colt Frontier Single Action, the legendary "Peacemaker" (right)

Bottom. Among the century's more significant long arms were (from top) the Henry Rifle, Sharps carbine, and Hall flintlock

iel Wesson had served as plant superintendent for Volcanic, which became the New Haven Arms Company, maker of one of the 1860s' legendary arms, the Henry Rifle. The name changed again in 1866 to one that would endure: Winchester.

With the arrival of plentiful (but never inexpensive) whale oil, our late eighteenth–early nineteenth-century predecessors enjoyed a reasonably bright and smokeless lamp for the first time. Lard was much cheaper, and a reasonable substitute. Patented lard lamps, and devices burning turpentine-base fuel proliferated through the 1840s and '50s. But as late as 1852, a new whale-oil railway conductor's lantern was patented and manufactured.

A few visionaries demonstrated other alternatives: Sir Humphrey Davy snapped on the electric arc light in 1808. Independently, Michael Faraday and Joseph Henry approximated the first electric generators around 1831. Curiously, Faraday had hit upon the idea of an electric motor ten years before; it had to wait for the generator. Vermont blacksmith Thomas Davenport began building electric motors in 1834. By the late 1830s, we had the protoprocesses of electroplating and telegraphy.

The telegraph, properly the electromagnetic telegraph, belongs in that small and rare cluster of supremely important technical innovations. Like the search for an efficient artificial light, the desire for rapid long-distance communication was as old as humankind. By the end of the eighteenth century, we were scarcely further along than the ancient Greeks with their beacon fires. In 1790s France, a mechanical telegraph—a semaphore system mounted on high towers—offered some improvement. But already such now-forgotten pioneers as Geneva's George LeSage had begun experimenting with the idea of electrical telegraphy. The names of such early nineteenth-century scientists as Volta, Ampère, Wheatstone, and Ohm became lodged in the terminology of electrical science.

Yet it remained for an American professional artist, Samuel F. B. Morse, to gather up the known elements, fuse them into a practical system, and then produce the public-relations flourish to get telegraphy moving. Morse patented his system in 1837, and squeezed an appropriation from Congress to set up a line between Washington and Baltimore. In 1844, with his assistant Alfred Vail at the other end, Morse transmitted the imperishable rhetorical question, "What hath God wrought!?"

It was a simple system, requiring a single line (the earth completed the electrical circuit), an electromagnet that would click when the circuit was broken according to a code, and a switch or "key" to control the circuit. The 1840s and '50s brought a frantic race to build a telegraphy network, and after the English Channel was spanned in 1851, American paper merchant Cyrus Field began a long, generous, and difficult process of laying the first

Opposite. Cased accouterments for the hunter: a detail of this handsome mid-nineteenth-century percussion sporting weapon, twin barrels detached to demonstrate its configuration as a rifle-shotgun, attests to the considerable skill of maker William Wingert of Detroit. The lacquered powder flask, with measuring spout, was a fixture of the late muzzle-loading age

Invented by Philadelphian George Clymer in 1815, the Columbian press received a better reception in Britain than in the United States. The museum's 1857 model was made in London

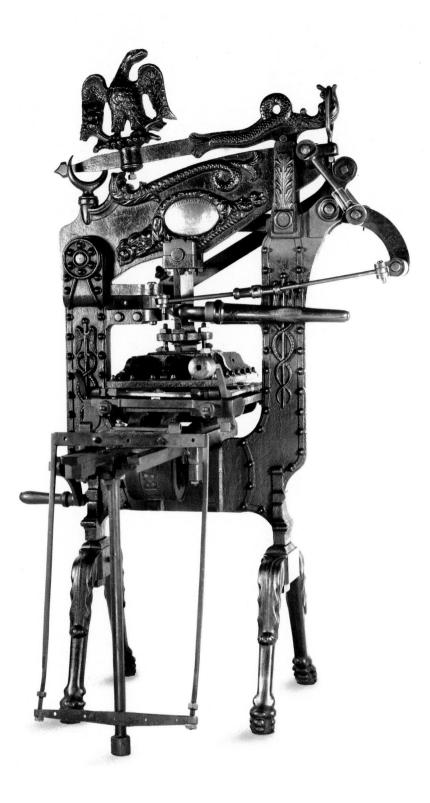

transocean cable. After crushing setbacks, Field finally completed in 1858 a cable between Newfoundland and Ireland. The first message, from Queen Victoria to President James Buchanan, was received by a galvanometer, used in laboratories to measure small electrical currents. The old brass-faced instrument, in a wooden box resting on a Rococo revival base, is a standout among the museum's huge collection of historic relics of early communication, as is a section of the original Atlantic cable. (As one of history's frustrating anticlimaxes, the cable soon failed. It would be 1866 before a permanent link with Europe was forged.)

The nineteenth century began with the printing craft about as Gutenberg had left it several centuries before. The crude, slow, wood-framed press manned by a "puller" at the bar (a big torsion screw) and a "beater" (applying ink to type from leather-covered balls) was still the world's only source of the printed word. Then, in 1813, an American carpenter and engineer, George Clymer of Philadelphia, lifted the press out of the Middle Ages by building a radically new machine. Clymer's all-iron press replaced the clumsy screw with a power stroke delivered through compound levers. The puller's stroke at the bar was thus more efficiently converted to vertical pressure on the platen. Peculiarly, and in apparent contradiction to the era's general acceptance of mechanical improvements, Clymer's Columbian press elicited yawns from tradition-minded printers, who thought it too expensive. Clymer moved to England, where his invention was so appreciated that he died rich in less than twenty years. The museum's Columbian is a masterpiece of voluptuous, ornate ironwork, proudly enhancing its mechanical merits.

While Clymer's press was an improvement, it remained for another American, Richard Hoe of New York, to yank the printing trade fully into the modern age. Hoe first pioneered flatbed and cylinder presses, and then around 1846 built the first rotary press in the United States, soon to print the *Philadelphia Public Ledger* at quadruple the speed formerly possible. Thus dawned the age of steam-powered, high-speed printing presses. It required only the adoption of continuously feeding rolls of paper, which occurred around the time of the Civil War, to complete the revolution, a fundamental change in mass communications. The improvements in presswork demanded comparable upgrading of composition techniques, but the age-old printer, hand-picking type at his "case," still had a few years remaining. It would be the 1880s before a Baltimore watchmaker, German-born Ottmar Mergenthaler, began building his famous, indestructible, slightly deranged-looking Linotypes.

The demand for small-shop printing equipment was strong, and Hoe made a popular hand press called the "Washington" in the years before the Civil War. One example displayed by the museum has a swashbuckling history. First used by a Louisiana newspaper to help elect Zachary Taylor president in 1848, it was shipped to California during the Gold Rush (after crossing the Isthmus of Panama, being dumped in a jungle stream, and printing a Panamanian newspaper) and hauled through a succession of California and Nevada boom towns. One of its owners printed a newspaper so stridently pro-Union, in a town of Confederate leanings, that the press received an armed guard. In 1862, in Aurora, Nevada, the man at the Hoe was young Samuel Clemens. Bret Harte was another pressman in the old machine's picaresque past.

Eastern America, with its many swift rivers tumbling off the Appalachian uplands, was made to order for water-powered industry. Millwright Oliver Evans of Delaware had succeeded as a late eighteenth-century industrialist by applying innovative thinking to the flour-milling business. Moving to Philadelphia and turning to steam power, Evans became America's first great steam pioneer. He built our first successful high-pressure factory engine, and thus pointed the way to far greater power generation than was possible with the low-pressure units familiar since the days of Newcomen and Watt. Evans even experimented with self-propelled vehicles, and in 1805 built a steam dredge that moved under its own power, and is generally considered to be America's first self-propelled vehicle. In all, he built about fifty engines before his death in 1819. The museum displays a rare document on one of them, dated 1812, outlining sales and operation terms for an installation in Marietta, Ohio. The new Grasshopper beam engine was rated at twenty horsepower, Evans said—"the power of a horse to be rated at 150 pounds raised perpendicularly 220 feet per minute."

In the year of Napoleon's first exile, 1814, a French chemist named Joseph Nicéphore Niepce began experimenting with the materials of photography. Silver nitrate was the key: its habit of turning dark in the sun seemed promising and had lured many dabblers for almost one hundred years. As early as 1822, Niepce produced his first positive image on an exposed metal plate, and in 1829 joined forces with another Frenchman working along similar lines, Louis J. M. Daguerre, a physicist who also painted popular stage sets. Niepce died in 1833, but in 1837 Daguerre perfected their process wherein a polished metal plate, coated with silver iodide, was exposed in a focused camera and developed with mercury vapor to produce a realistic image. Daguerre sold his process to the French government, which gave it to the world in 1839.

An Englishman, William H. F. Talbot, meanwhile was making similar—in some ways more sophisticated—strides. Talbot, using paper soaked with silver chloride, made negative images first, and from them, positives. Talbot's system was actually reported before Daguerre's, but it did not catch on, although it more clearly forecast the future of photography by its ability to make any number of positive prints from one negative.

The Daguerreotype was an immediate sensation, and was enthusiastically pioneered in the United States by Samuel F. B. Morse. Around 1851, the wet-plate or collodion process introduced glass negatives capable of astonishing sensitivity to detail, which in the hands of masters like Mathew B. Brady and Alexander Gardner left us haunting reminders of the middle nineteenth century. The museum is deep in equipment from photography's cradle years, including a complete camera, tripod, and necessary laboratory equipment made by A. Schurtz in Paris. Early cameras tend to look alike, surprisingly standardized, because the form had been established long before as the *camera obscura,* or dark chamber. Artists since the Renaissance had used it for precise composition, or tracing.

Such equipment was superbly made. Mid-nineteenth-century lenses are masterpieces of machined brass, their inner optics moving smoothly to focus by the twist of a knurled knob, driving a rack and pinion. Tripods and wooden camera boxes were of high-quality cabinetry. Special posing chairs featured a garrote-like head clamp to keep the squirm-prone subject from moving.

The fascination of our ancestors with the new process is revealed less by the device than by the works it produced. The museum displays many examples of the portrait rage that swept the 1850s and '60s, when we showered each other with our pictures printed on *cartes de visite.* Other portrait prints were framed in small, lidded gutta percha cases, which enjoyed an explosion of popularity in the 1850s. One of the museum's rarest relics of the genre is an 1851 Daguerreotype of a thoughtful-looking four-year-old, the earliest likeness of Thomas Alva Edison.

Thomas Edison would become one of the most photographed men of his time, but his 1851 sitting with a Daguerreotypist—at age four—was probably his first encounter with a camera

*a*s the Conestoga wagon entered its years of decline, another type of horse-drawn vehicle was in the ascendancy. The famous Concord coach first rolled out of the New Hampshire shop of Abbot & Downing in 1827, and soon was in service across the United States. Some reached South America, South Africa, and even Australia. Rugged and fast, and perhaps a bit less wretchedly uncomfortable than most public conveyances of the time, Concords carried between six and sixteen passengers, depending on construction, and were pulled by teams of four or six horses. Stage companies (the "stage" was any point where horses were regularly changed) competed furiously for passengers, and used the larger or mail-style Concords, of which the museum has a colorful example. Built around 1865, it carried passengers and mail for decades between York, Maine, and Portsmouth, New Hampshire. Around 1910, it became a hotel coach for the Kearsarge House in Portsmouth, shuttling guests from the depot. In its original faded red paint, with floral furbelows in gold, the old Concord fairly exudes the glamour that marked this supremely American vehicle.

Not all the museum's horse-drawn conveyances have wheels: a selection of sleighs demonstrates the vanished world of Albany and Portland cutters, Boston boobies and work sleighs, and even a pre-Revolutionary pung sleigh. A graceful Albany cutter of 1840 once glided through the New England

snows bearing Daniel Webster and John Greenleaf Whittier. One of the museum's most beautiful vehicles is an Albany cutter from the peak ornamental year of 1865, a masterpiece of elegance with its curved red body, gilt with yellow floral trim, and carved birds' heads thrusting forward. A high curved dash with leather wings deflected snow tossed by a horse's feet.

By the 1840s, American fire engines were handsome pumpers whose elaborate ornamentation is repeated on their distant heirs to this day. The museum is well stocked with such early, hand-drawn, hand-pumped machines. A Hunneman of 1840 demonstrates the New England style of pumper, while an Agnew of similar age reveals the different pump style of the Philadelphia school. Such machines had long histories of use: the Agnew Eagle was built for the city of Pittsburgh in 1843, and concluded its service in a small volunteer company in Ohio in 1928. Hand-drawn, hand-pumped machines were still being manufactured for small towns long after the debut of great horse-drawn steam pumpers. The museum shows an 1873 hand-pumper, made by L. Button & Son of Waterford, New York, that served in a historic fire at Haverhill, Massachusetts, in 1882.

The brave firemen, trundling their pumper and hose reel through fire-showered streets, formed an enduring image in American folklore. But the truth is that tradition-minded firemen resisted innovative equipment. Steam-powered fire pumps were available as early as 1829 in England. In 1841, New York City firemen disputed the insurance companies' advocacy of power equipment. But by the 1850s it was clear that the benefits of steam pumps could no longer be withheld. One excellent example of the early type is a Cole Brothers engine, made in Pawtucket, Rhode Island, c. 1870. A classical beauty of mid-Victorian steam engineering, the horse-drawn Cole would pump as much as six hundred gallons per minute.

We may properly wonder why our ancestors required so much time to invent even the crudest forerunner of the bicycle. Astonishingly, the French had already been soaring the skies for nearly ten years when one of their countrymen, the Comte de Sivrac, built the pioneering two-wheeler, in 1791. The count's riding pleasure was limited, for he neglected to include a steering mechanism. Little else happened until 1818, when a German forester named Karl von Drais built a steerable bike to help speed up his rounds through the woods. Like the earlier version, the Draisine (also called the "hobby horse") had no pedals, and the rider simply pushed the ground with his feet and coasted. Knowing a clever innovation when they saw one, the style-conscious fops of England rushed to obtain hobby horses. But England's merciless cartoonists made such savage sport of the new fad that it lasted only two years. Thus the first wave of biking aborted in embarrassment as one of history's most complete false starts. The museum displays a rare original example of the first type of bicycle, by an unknown European maker around 1818. Its iron-tired, solid wood wheels are lightened by heart-shaped cutouts.

Opposite. Polished brass and carved, gilded scrolls embellish this detail of a hand pumper, built by John Agnew in the Philadelphia style in 1843

Above. Firefighting equipment of early nineteenth-century New England featured lots of buckets

In another way, too, the English example stands for the might-have-beens of nineteenth-century travel. The British went on a road-building spree just after the Napoleonic wars, and in the 1820s and '30s a spectacular congeries of steam-powered commercial highway coaches was chuffing between many cities and towns. Some of the vehicles were reasonably successful, and their safety record surprisingly good. But savage opposition by the railways, horse-drawn-coach interests, and suspicious farmers combined to drive the steamers out of business, assisted by British satirical cartoonists directing their genius for invective at the admittedly bizarre-looking road monsters.

No such developments enlivened the American road, which was simply too long and in too wretched a condition. Canals, and then railroads, received most of America's transportation development energy in the nineteenth century. After imported British locomotives proved unsuitable, Americans began building their own around 1830, when the Tom Thumb raced a horse at Baltimore, and the Best Friend went into service at Charleston, South Carolina. America's third successful train was the De Witt Clinton. In 1831, its festive first run, carrying five cars jammed with passengers, was a round trip between Albany and Schenectady, New York, on the fledgling Mohawk & Hudson Railroad. The locomotive was designed by John B. Jervis, chief engineer of the West Point Foundry, and built by David Matthew, who bravely manned the throttle on the maiden run and achieved the respectable speed of thirty miles per hour. As nobody of that day knew what a railway passenger coach should be, the builders took the practical expedient of clapping stagecoach bodies onto heavy frames with flanged iron wheels.

Alas, the Clinton vanished in the last century, and the one displayed at the museum is not original. But neither is it a modern reproduction. In 1893, the New York Central re-created the little train very accurately for display at the Columbian Exposition. The new Clinton worked so well the Central used it for years for public-relations purposes before finally donating it to the museum in 1935. Thus the reincarnated train enjoyed its own career, and already has lived far longer than the original.

Opposite. The 1831 DeWitt Clinton (not the original, but an accurate replica of the 1890s) provides a sharp contrast with its stablemate of 1941, the mighty C&O Allegheny

Top. The 1818 Draisine is considered the first steerable riding machine. The maker of the museum's example is unknown

Bottom. The Albany cutter, whose development began around 1819, was one of the century's most graceful productions

Lights
Come on
at
Menlo Park

*e*arly Victorians liked their machinery to manifest the aesthetics of their time. One of the museum's largest stationary steam engines is a masterwork of such Gothic revival shapes as peaked arches, quatre-foils, and fluted columns, altogether forming a power plant in the image of a cathedral. When installed at a Philadelphia factory around 1855, glistening in its original deep green paint with red and gold trim, the great engine was indeed the altar of a new age. Its flywheel, eighteen feet in diameter, turned at a stately thirty revolutions per minute. For almost eighty years the engine faithfully generated its 200 horsepower.

Tentative attribution credits the Novelty Iron Works of New York City with the creation of this beauty. A clouded birth certificate for major machinery of the era is unusual, as well as unfortunate, for the proud builders usually emblazoned all vital statistics on prominent brass plates. Some once-famous names, forgotten by all but students of the history of power, appear on the flanks of machines that powered American industry through the Civil War. One of the greatest names was George Henry Corliss of Providence, Rhode Island, who had patented one of the earliest sewing machines before going on to become a renowned steam engineer. Corliss built engines of cherished efficiency, first for the New England textile industry, and after 1856 under his own name. His innovations included an automatic cut-off and a valve gear. The museum's Corliss-attributed engines

Opposite. Here, in the heart of the Menlo Park laboratory, Edison and his staff worked during the great inventor's most productive period. Between 1876 and 1886 came more than 400 patented inventions, including the incandescent lamp and the phonograph

include specimens of 1859 and 1888. Not only did they work well, but Corliss engines led the way toward clean, purposeful mechanical design.

Such stationary steam engines could be built in a wide range of sizes, and most were meant to be firmly bolted down. But the need for semiportable power was strong, and it was met by manufacturers like the Blandy Brothers of Zanesville, Ohio. From the 1850s through the rest of the century, the Blandys built an enormously popular line of "skid" engines, such as the museum's 1860 model of five horsepower, a portable power plant especially good for sawmills. The company also made the sawmill to go with their engine.

Among the demonstrations of period life that are regularly in progress in Greenfield Village, the actual operation of a number of steam engines creates a sense of industrial verisimilitude. There, unlike the still, cold ranks of museum exhibits, old engines work daily. At the Armington and Sims Machine Shop, a C. H. Brown & Co. engine from more than a century ago whirs its butter-smooth way, cheerfully popping *pft-phfft* from its visceral valves. The same action occurs at the Loranger Gristmill, where an 1870 Davis powers the actual grinding of grain (demonstrating, for those sensitive to the finer points of industrial history, the milling innovations of the great Oliver Evans). The village's Tripp Sawmill and Stony Creek Sawmill exhibit the power of steam as well as the changing technology of American board-cutting, respectively, from up and down blades to circular saws.

Beautiful and rich in personality they may have been, but steam engines had their limitations. For one, their boilers blew up with disturbing frequency under careless tending. They were also expensive. And for all their impressive size, they were relatively puny for the Western world's increasingly power-hungry industries. Other energy forms began to emerge. France's Etienne Lenoir created the first production internal combustion engine (fueled by illuminating gas) in 1860, but it failed. Germany's Nicolaus Otto and Eugen Langen built more than three thousand improved versions from 1866 to 1876, whereupon Otto hit upon the power plant that would change the world again: the four-cycle compression engine, which ran either on gas or gasoline. The museum displays various examples of early one-cylinder Otto engines, all of them of supreme significance in the development of power. Perhaps the best is an 1877 Otto, water cooled, with a fifty-three-inch flywheel.

Although Otto's engine was first used as a stationary power source, the most provocative thing about it was its adaptability to new forms of transportation. Replacement of the piston steam engine would come most satisfactorily from the steam turbine, first built to operating standards by Sir Charles A. Parsons of England in 1884. The heat-ignition Diesel, too, would soon come along as a factory power plant, as well as branching out into motive power. Rudolf Diesel, its German inventor, was typical of a small but significant group of new engineers, university trained, replacing

Opposite. In this general view of the museum's steam engine collection, the large wheel at the left marks an 1859 engine by George Henry Corliss. The wheel is twenty-four feet in diameter; the total engine weighs 80,000 pounds

Above. Scale model of a steeple compound marine steam engine, built in 1872, demonstrates a then-popular power plant used in Great Lakes vessels. The museum also has a full-sized version

the self-taught tinkerers and natural geniuses who had led the mechanical parade up to then. Theoretical science merged with mechanics, creating the technological setting for the twentieth century. Already there was, by the 1880s and '90s, a different *look* to the power machinery displayed in the museum and Greenfield Village. The big twin Diesel of 1898, built only one year after the type's introduction after five years of development, seems all-business; as unsentimental as, well, a Diesel.

Increasingly high on the coveted list of things to master was that tantalizing genie, electricity. A few steam-driven generators appeared in the 1850s, and one actually powered an arc light in a lighthouse. But the major breakthrough waited for 1867, when Zenobe T. Gramme produced the pioneering modern generator, a rotary concoction of ring-wound armature and field coil. Gramme very practically installed arc lights in his Paris factory in 1870. Other arc installations occurred in France and Germany in the early 1870s, but the first commercial United States use came in 1878 at Wanamaker's in Philadelphia, and was directed by C. F. Brush, who also installed street arc lights in Cleveland in 1879. Arc lamps had been demonstrated at the Philadelphia Centennial Exposition in 1876. In 1877, Thomas Edison, aged 30, focused his formidable energies on developing a more satisfactory electric light.

In his childhood back in Milan, Ohio, and Port Huron, Michigan, Edison's prospects seemed meager; he was both sickly and mischievous, to the point of being troublesome beyond the norm. His formal education ended after a few months when his teacher expelled him as "addled," and suggested he be taught farming. His mother, an ex-teacher herself, disagreed, and taught him at home, encouraging his intense curiosity. At twelve, already growing deaf, he took his first railroad job, hawking newspapers and snacks on a passenger train. And at fifteen, he became a telegrapher.

Edison's first job was on the Grand Trunk Railway of Ontario, Canada. He soon returned to the United States in 1863, and spent the next six years drifting through the Midwest and Northeast, always in jobs related to that communications marvel of the age, the telegraph. Landing in Boston at twenty, he began free-lance tinkering with telegraphic equipment, and in 1868 received his first patent, an electric vote recorder for legislative bodies. Brashly carrying his invention to a Congressional committee in Washington, he was crushed to learn that any thought of speeding up the voting tally was anathema to the representatives, who would have been deprived of the convenience of vote trading during their customary long roll call. Edison resolved never again to invent anything impractical and for which there was no commercial potential.

He moved to New York at twenty-two and almost immediately struck gold, improving the crude stock tickers of the day so dramatically that in only a year, in 1870, he was paid $40,000 for his new patents. Edison set up a new laboratory in Newark, New Jersey, made stock tickers, worked as a

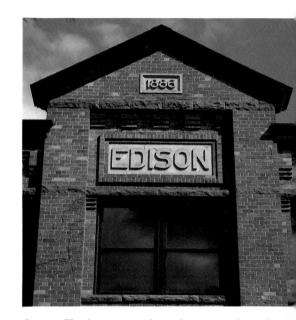

Opposite. This direct current electric fan was manufactured by Thomas A. Edison, Inc., of West Orange, New Jersey

Above. The Edison Illuminating Company building in Greenfield Village reproduced the original 1886 structure in Detroit, where Henry Ford worked as a young plant engineer. Inside are period boilers, steam engines, and a historic dynamo named Jumbo

consultant for the Western Union Company, and saved enough money in six years to build a complex of buildings in a rural section of New Jersey called Menlo Park. For the next decade, in the world's first industrial research and development laboratory, Edison directed a golden age of practical invention. At Menlo Park he aimed for a minor invention every ten days; something big every six months. In ten years he obtained 420 patents (of his lifetime total of 1,093), including those for the phonograph and electric light, supreme achievements of the Wizard of Menlo Park. Joseph Swan of Great Britain actually beat him to the carbon filament bulb by one year. But Edison's greater achievement was his rapid development of a power distribution system: the supporting network of generators, meters, and wires without which any lightbulb would flicker dimly, if at all.

The museum displays an odd-looking, homely, six-foot-tall device suggesting equipment in Dr. Frankenstein's laboratory. But this relic deserves a place in any pantheon of electrical rarities. It is an original Edison bipolar dynamo from his first commercial electrical system, in 1880. Curiously, the system went to sea, for it was installed aboard the S. S. *Columbia*, a new ship that sailed from New York around Cape Horn to San Francisco with 115 incandescent lights blazing all the way. Called "Long-legged Mary Anne" because of its awkward, stalky look, the dynamo would soon recede in the design of newer generations of bipolars.

Of equal and perhaps greater significance is the artifact known as Jumbo Dynamo Number 9, the sole survivor from Edison's Pearl Street Station in New York City, generally acknowledged as the country's first central electric station. Jumbo stands with other early equipment in the Edison Illuminating Company building in Greenfield Village, an exhibit reproducing a late nineteenth-century power station. The original began operations September 4, 1882, with Jumbo Number 9 the first generator to be set humming. Including its Armington and Sims steam engine, the generator weighs more than 60,000 pounds, and can still produce its original quota of 100 kilowatts.

One good reason Jumbo remained in such immaculate condition is that its working career was relatively short. It represented the system of direct current, of which Edison was unaccountably fond, and which soon proved something of a dead end. Direct current was uneconomical for transmission beyond short range, while alternating current could be sent afar via high-voltage transmission and transformers. George Westinghouse, a great early rival of Edison and founder of the Westinghouse Company of Pittsburgh, locked up the relevant patents. When electricity started flowing from the mighty new Niagara Falls hydroelectric plant in 1895, it served a rapidly expanding North American power grid irrevocably stamped AC.

Menlo Park itself is, in sum, the weightiest artifact in the Henry Ford Museum/Greenfield Village complex. A seedbed of change that would affect every American, the Edison buildings are paramount in both tech-

Opposite. Edison's "Jumbo Dynamo Number 9" was installed in New York City in 1882; in perfect condition today, it stands in the Edison Illuminating Company building in Greenfield Village

nological and social history. The reconstructed 1876 laboratory, a two-story weatherboarded structure, is the soul of the complex. The first floor combines the original machine shop, chemical laboratory, office, and the legendary cubbyhole where Edison took his catnaps. The rooms and their relics are maintained to suggest the scene of December 31, 1879, when Edison here made his first public demonstration of incandescent light. Upstairs, where the inventor did most of his work, the era suggested is earlier. The long, gas-lit room—its walls lined with ancient bottles of chemicals—holds the core of Edison's greatest work. Here is the vote recorder that fizzled in 1868, and the stock ticker that clicked in 1869. The curious-looking electric pen of 1875 is, once explained, quite clearly the origin of the mimeograph. His massive contributions to early telephone technology are revealed by such inventions as his 1879 "loudspeaking receiver."

Edison's favorite creation was the phonograph, displayed in its earliest production form of 1878. The recording medium, tinfoil, worked just the same as a number of materials since then, from wax to vinyl. Everything that has happened to the phonograph since 1877 has been mere embellishment on the primal idea Edison demonstrated that December 4, playing back his own recitation of *Mary Had a Little Lamb*. Meantime, he was proceeding on his work toward artificial light. Something of a latecomer to the tantalizing dream, he felt that others' known approach—seeking a short, heavy, low-resistant filament—was the wrong way. Moreover, he rejected the prevailing notion that all lights on a circuit should work at once. Thus he successfully strove for a thin, high-resistance filament for bulbs that could be turned on and off individually. Carbonized cotton sewing thread was the first successful answer to the filament problem, although the Edison crew would make a number of materials work. For the great test of New Year's Eve, 1879, the filament used was carbonized paper.

By then, Edison's booming research and development operation had far outstripped the original laboratory building. A new brick machine shop, built in 1878, was crucial to the development of Edison's lighting plans, serving as power plant for the first centralized system in which not only the laboratory but also three Menlo Park residences were illuminated. The machine shop also made the original models for all the new apparatus: the dynamos, meters, fuses, and sockets that had never existed before. The reconstructed building contains, among much original equipment and materials, the very steam boiler that supplied the historic first night's power.

More than half a dozen Menlo Park buildings stand in Greenfield Village; most original are the little glass-blowing house, where the first bulbs were made, and the Sarah Jordan Boarding House. Many of Edison's twenty-odd machinists, draftsmen, chemists, patternmakers, and others were young and unmarried, and Mrs. Jordan's was their home. The boarding house is the only completely original building to survive of those first wired for light, and stands today, with replica bulbs and exposed wiring, as

Opposite. The Menlo Park laboratory, the "invention factory" in New Jersey where Thomas Edison conducted his most significant work, was reconstructed in Greenfield Village. Edison himself returned here in triumph in 1929, fifty years after he first successfully demonstrated his incandescent lighting system

Top. A 1912 Model T Ford waits at the Sarah Jordan Boarding House, which accommodated a number of Edison's employees—mostly young bachelors. It is one of the most original of all the Menlo Park structures moved to Greenfield Village. In this house, on New Year's Day 1879, Edison demonstrated his new lighting system

Bottom. Architectural detail, Sarah Jordan House

it did in 1879. An ideal companion piece to the shop-and-laboratory atmosphere of other Menlo buildings, Mrs. Jordan's reveals the human or social side of Edison's staff and their mid-Victorian era, and in a broader sense evokes the atmosphere of a once-essential institution that has all but vanished.

In ten years, Menlo Park was obsolete. In 1886 Edison began moving everything to West Orange, New Jersey, where he built the largest, best-equipped laboratory on earth, ten times larger than Menlo. Here he developed his Kinetograph, or motion picture camera, and Kinetoscope, a sort of peep-show projector. In 1893, he began filming motion pictures in the first movie studio. Also at West Orange Edison fully developed the phonograph, and sent it forth to sensational commercial success. The big complex is represented by the very building where Edison's version of the disc phonograph was born in 1912. Still another Greenfield Village building from the inventor's later period is the laboratory from his winter headquarters in Fort Myers, Florida, where Edison worked some forty years.

The Edison Illuminating Company building (shelter for Jumbo) is, not entirely by chance, a small replica of the Detroit electrical plant where Henry Ford worked as a young engineer. At a company convention in Atlantic City, Ford met Edison and encouraged him to continue his pioneer automotive tinkering. They were cut from the same cloth: practical, systematic, goal-oriented, inventive, visionary, and doubtless eccentric. Later generations would denigrate some of their methods and viewpoints. It was clearly a mistake for Edison to cling to the principle of direct current after alternating current was demonstrated best, and perhaps he might have accomplished even more with a greater willingness to substitute abstract calculations for his favored pragmatic experimentation. But such imperfections were trivial indeed when set against the mighty works of the Wizard of Menlo Park, whose life changed the world.

*b*y the middle of the nineteenth century, New England had surpassed Great Britain as the center of machine tool manufacture. Such Civil War era shop tools as the museum's 1855 C. W. Eddy screw-cutting lathe would seem almost modern, were it not for such ornamental touches as claw feet. Only a medium-sized lathe of the time, it nevertheless carried a forty-one-inch face plate and a five-step cone pulley, rack-and-pinion traverse, and two-and-one-half-inch lead screw. Low slung and massive on its animal feet, the nine-foot machine has a rhinoceros-like solidity. Another important relic is an 1860 planer from the Putnam Machine Company of Fitchburg, Massachusetts. Designed to shape iron and steel mold blocks for a manufacturing company, the planer is an assured blend of function and Rococo revival styling. A machine designed for woodworking shops is the nine-foot Gray and Woods planer of c. 1865, considered a milestone in speed and convenience.

Even the most amateurish home craftsman of today should recognize (and soon master) the museum's red-painted 1875 Carey jointer, an essential woodworking device whose graceful design has remained nearly unchanged for more than a century. The museum specimen was probably used in making wagon bodies. Nearby stands a phalanx of pioneer milling machines, a family second only to the lathe in machine-shop usefulness. By 1880, the milling machine was essentially in its modern form, a future seen in the Cincinnati Milling Machine of 1881, an efficient metal remover with a rotating cutter. Such machines, perfected for the major industrial jobs of the nineteenth century, merely grew larger and more complex in the twentieth.

Some of the best stationary steam engines—including Edison's first power plants—were made by the Armington and Sims Company. Henry Ford honored the name by applying it to the fully operational machine shop and foundry in Greenfield Village, which demonstrates a turn-of-the-century job shop. Such establishments made the machinery used in specialized, mass production factories, and were essential to industry.

No better place exists to sense the mysterious beauty of metalworking than amid these 1890s lathes, boring mills, planers, and slotters in the Armington and Sims shop. The sounds in the spacious building are partially foreign to the modern ear. From the adjoining power house, a giant leather belt drives the overhead power shafts that hang from the ceiling, up beside the long roof lantern of windows, going *cheepity clack, cheepity clack*. Looped and straight leather belts, for forward and reverse, angle down to the machines. The not-unpleasant scents of grease, oil, and freshly shaved iron and steel mingle with those of foursquare oak office furniture in the open front office. In a thousand such settings, the Industrial Revolution found its vocabulary, and made its rules.

Land-based telegraphy was well established long before the Civil War, but the exigencies of that conflict honed the skill and speed of engineers and operators alike. The museum displays a definitive collection of early equipment, including beautifully made keys and receivers, and strange-looking primary cells that were the only sources of power. Such glass jars, containing carbon and zinc electrodes in electrochemical reaction, were linked together in series. The arrangement soon produced its own colloquial term: the battery.

The telephone, like the telegraph and electric light, might be described as an invention by a committee, each member working independently. The invention would ultimately be realized by the one whose synthesis of elements worked best. For the telephone, that man was Alexander Graham Bell, although a German schoolteacher, J. Phillip Reis, deserves to be mentioned in the same breath for his partially successful "Das Telefon" of 1860. Bell, in 1875 and '76, made rapid progress in his invention while seeking

Left and above. The Armington and Sims Machine Shop, erected in Greenfield Village in 1928, was based on engine- and machine-making factories of the late 1800s, and incorporated features of the original A&S plant in Providence, Rhode Island. As a functioning shop today, it is powered by a nineteenth-century steam engine that drives an overhead shaft and belt system, operating lathes, planers, shapers, drill presses, and other period metalworking machinery

ways to aid the deaf, and a replica of the model that received American history's most valuable patent is displayed in the museum's enormous communications collection. In terms of use, the most significant artifact may be Bell's 1877 box telephone, the first commercial model ever installed, linking a Boston banker's home and office. A hole in the wooden box served as both transmitter and receiver, requiring quick shifts from mouth to ear. The device was probably made by Bell's near-legendary assistant, Thomas Watson. A signaling button on the box lives in telephone history as the "Watson thumper."

Soon the first commercial switchboards were in production, and the museum displays an 1878 model on which the "plug and jack" system is already developed. A directory of 1878 adds to the aura of communications history around the old board. The earliest known dial telephone bestows immortality on its implausible inventor, a Kansas City funeral director. Almon B. Strowger's first automatic telephone went into service in LaPorte, Indiana, in 1892; today the nickel-plated dial and black mouthpiece and receiver of the museum's example are clear evidence that Mr. Strowger commanded the telephone of the future.

Invention of the typewriter was even more of a group effort, going back to at least 1714 in England, patented in 1829 in America, and improved in France in 1833. But the first commercially successful model was created in 1868 by the team of Christopher L. Sholes, Carlos Glidden, and Samuel Soulé. They persuaded Philo Remington, the Ilion, New York, arms tycoon, to add typewriters as another sideline (he was already making sewing machines), and the first thousand machines were made in 1874. The museum's huge collection of typewriters begins with one of the pioneers, a "Remington-Sholes."

With the typewriter in place, other office equipment could not be far behind. Edison's "electric pen" heralded the mimeographs of 1888 and 1897. His phonographs spawned the dictation equipment industry, all traced in the museum's displays. The first general-purpose calculator to achieve commercial success was the 1888 comptometer of Felt and Tarrant, which could add, subtract, multiply, and divide. The museum's spindly but still serviceable example dates c. 1896.

For about five decades, photography was in the hands of professionals and scientists. An aura of necromancy surrounded the photographer, who from his wagon-borne portable studio and darkroom fiddled with strange machines, mixed occult chemicals, disappeared into total darkness, and emerged with magical results. Then in the late 1870s, young George Eastman experimented successfully with dry-plate processes. Suddenly the need for instant development was gone, and with it the need for portable darkrooms.

Eastman was just starting. He produced the first practical roll film in 1884 by applying a light-sensitive emulsion to a collodion-coated paper

Opposite. From the dawn of production typewriters, the middle 1870s, comes this Remington Model Number 1, invented by Christopher Sholes and associates. Its users could print only capitals

Above. The nineteenth century's second half brought a stunning transition: photography leaped from the age of the wet-plate studio camera (example at left dates from the 1860s) to George Eastman's Kodak, of which an 1888 model—with suitable advertising—rests on the marble-top table

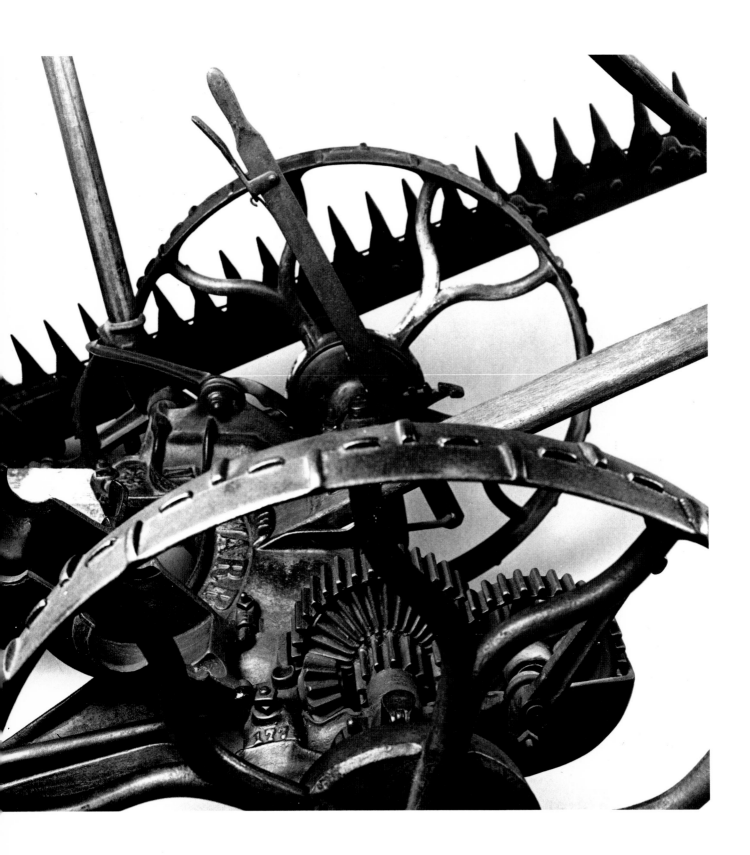

first, later switching to celluloid. In 1888, Eastman introduced the first Kodak, incorporating a roll holder developed by W. H. Walker. The hand-held, $25 box camera was loaded at the factory for a staggering one hundred pictures. When all the roll was exposed, the customer sent the camera back to Eastman's factory for a $10 processing, printing, and reloading. The camera's lens and shutter were preset. "You press the button," said the inventor's advertising, "we do the rest." Think of it. Almost overnight, the arcane specialty of photography was released to the multitude. Anyone could make pictures.

New models came quickly. The first pocket Kodak arrived in the 1890s, as did the first of the still-remembered bellows cameras. The museum displays them in bewildering profusion. Many were presented to Henry Ford by George Eastman himself.

Eadweard Muybridge, a flamboyant early photographer, has at least partial claim to the title of father of motion pictures. In about 1870, Muybridge photographed racehorses in motion with a series of cameras, then built a revolving viewer that displayed the photographs as animation. Others worked on the idea, too. Thomas Edison and his inventive group produced the real breakthrough in 1889 with the Kinetograph and Kinetoscope; an 1896 version of the Edison camera is displayed. It remained only for two French brothers, Louis and Auguste Lumière, to patent the cinematograph, the first true motion picture projector, in 1895.

Halfway through the nineteenth century, although the reaper was virtually standard equipment, most of America's grain threshing was still performed in a manner that any reincarnated medieval peasant would have understood perfectly: beating with a hinged flail and winnowing from a shallow basket. Threshing had never been a particular problem, for grain, once cut, could be stored and threshed later, when the urgencies of harvest had passed. The 1780s had seen some experimentation with a boxed-in winnowing machine called the "Dutch fan," but its use was not widespread. Rapid developments occurred in the 1840s and '50s, however, and the mechanical thresher-separator became a reality. The new machines were so efficient as to usher in a new, enduring institution—the custom thresher-man, who freed individual farmers from the purchase and care of expensive equipment. One of the best early units was the Wheeler and Mellick, made in Albany, New York. Two horses on a treadmill provided power; worked by four men, Wheeler and Mellicks of the 1860s could thresh a respectable two hundred bushels of grain daily. The museum's 1866 model seems still able to handle its quota.

The Civil War years added new dynamics of change to the matter of farm mechanization. Commodity prices soared worldwide, and farm boys by the millions joined the army, creating both a labor shortage and a vast new market. Inventors and manufacturers released a new generation of more efficient machines. Starting with the 1860s, the museum's farm relics become dra-

Opposite. By about 1880, when this New Warrior mowing machine was built by the Warrior Mowing Company of Little Falls, New York, technology had already revolutionized American farming

Above. This 1916 Port Huron tractor once labored in Greenfield Village maintenance jobs, but was retired in the early 1950s. Volunteers recently restored it in the Armington & Sims Machine Shop, and—fully operational again—it chuffs regularly forth at Village special events

matically more complex. Grain drills, sulky plows, and twine binders suggest an increasing specialization. Altogether new was the reaper-binder of the 1870s. The museum's example of the complicated machine is by Walter A. Wood of New York, New York.

The design aesthetic was perhaps less important to farm machinery makers than to manufacturers in other fields, yet—Victorians to the core—makers brightened their products with red paint, and applied gold stripes and gaudy flourishes of scrollwork. Farm wagons echoed circus wagons. Some of the ironwork on post-Civil War equipment was magnificent, as demonstrated by the museum's Eureka mowing machine of 1880. The nation's commercial artists and lithographers battled it out for their machinery-making clients with spectacular trade catalogs. The Aultman & Taylor Company of Mansfield, Ohio, featured a comical starving rooster deprived of grain gleanings by superbly efficient threshers. The rival Rumely Company of La Porte, Indiana, countered with sentimental art of happy children playing beside streams, hay ricks, and threshers. The museum's archives bulge with such colorful material.

The first farm revolution added the power of horses to machinery, and the combination worked well. Yet from the beginning some visionaries thought steam engines might be preferable to horses. Curiously, it was nonindustrial Dixie where steam first took its stand on the farm, in the big central sugar mills and cotton gins, as early as the 1820s. One such mill is reconstructed in Greenfield Village. The Harahan Sugar Mill was built in Louisiana in 1845, beside the Mississippi River. Like others of the type, it employed a large, stationary steam engine, the same that spun factory wheels in the North. Why not create a small, portable steam engine to turn the working parts of threshing machines?

The first ones, resembling small locomotives on wagon wheels, were available by 1850. Paradoxically, this new producer of power could not move itself, and had to be towed around by horses, hardly inspiring the confidence to justify its high cost. But after twenty years the farm steamer began catching on. The museum has a gaggle of stovepipe-black specimens from the 1870s; they seem strangely capricious in design, like cartoonists' fancies, all spidery wheels and absurdly tall exhaust stacks, bristling with gauges, valves, rods, oilers, and flywheels. The museum's oldest example is also the most straightforward in design: a chunky little Owens, Lane & Dyer, built in 1870 in Hamilton, Ohio.

By the 1880s the first self-powered traction engines were chuffing majestically across the grain-farming horizons, towing the ungainly apparatus of the custom thresherman. The J. I. Case Company, founded in Racine, Wisconsin, in 1842, became the giant of the traction engine business. The museum's 1890 Case, with its graceful stack and magnificently filagreed gear wheel guard, may not be a thing of beauty, but is a joyful machine. In action, with its piston punching, governor whirling, and stack belching

Opposite. The beauty of nineteenth-century machinery shines in a detail view of a farm steam engine. This portable engine of 1882 was manufactured by Nichols, Shepard & Company of Battle Creek, Michigan

Above. The J. I. Case Company of Racine, Wisconsin, made this resplendent steam tractor in 1890

black coal smoke as it drove the shiny leather belt, slung in a long figure eight to the roaring thresher, the Case seemed the very soul of power to generations of farm youth. Sadly, such machines were always more bark than bite. The Case's fifteen horsepower is surpassed by many of today's home garden tractors. And while some were used in western fields for actual cultivation and harvest power, their unfavorable horsepower-to-weight ratio made them inefficient as moving power sources. At times they would ponderously dig themselves into holes.

*t*he mechanization of the American home moved rapidly after 1850. No sooner had American families accepted their first cook stove when manufacturers were ready with a new generation. The years just before, and especially just after, the Civil War were explosive with the development of mechanical appliances: apple parers, cherry pitters, coffee grinders, can openers, and egg beaters. The museum has them by the score. Detached from their original milieu such artifacts may seem lost and forlorn, but the museum's four model period kitchen displays are technologically informative, as well as nostalgically appealing. In the complete kitchen of c. 1890, the theme of change comes through strongest of all.

The major manufacturing centers of America's stove industry moved to the Midwest after 1850, and such leaders as the Michigan Stove Company of Detroit brought the American parlor stove to a vertex of efficiency and splendor. Michigan Stove's gigantic "Art Garland" emulates the conning tower of Captain Nemo's submarine: nickel-plated castings in swirling ocean waves embosom a doubledecker turret of iron grillwork, whose isinglass windows once radiated the cheery orange glow of burning coal. Made around 1898, the six-foot colossus represents the final flourishing of freestanding heating stoves as things of pride and glory. Central heating, pioneered before the Civil War and common since the 1870s, already had rendered such stoves obsolescent. Soon they would be passé embarrassments to the up-to-date homeowner.

By the time of the Civil War, sewing machines were becoming commonplace in the home. They assumed a special importance in the Confederacy, which was lacking in a garment industry and faced the task of clothing an army in the field. Sewing machines were moved into the South's churches, as women set up *de facto* factories where "nothing could be heard but the click of machines, the tearing of cloth, the ceaseless murmur of voices questioning," as one Virginia woman remembered. What sort of machines performed such service? As embodied in the museum's collection, they were sophisticated in engineering and superb in construction quality. More than that, they were beautiful in design and ornamentation. Together they constitute one of the museum's often overlooked great surprises, these jewellike creations of such forgotten names as Grover & Baker, Florence, Shaw

& Clark, and Wheeler & Wilson. Clearly, in producing their gleaming little machines—all shiny black enamel, gold-leaf scrolls, painted roses, mother-of-pearl inlay, polished hardwood cases, Rococo iron frames—the manufacturers aimed straight at the heart of Victorian decorative sensibilities. Why, then, do most Singers of the antebellum years appear as massively constructed factory machines? Because that is what they were. Isaac Singer began in 1850 as a maker of industrial machines, although soon his company joined the competitive home market, developed new marketing techniques, and grew to dominate the industry.

The nineteenth century's second half was a time of complexity in women's and children's fashions, often in adaptive imitation of styles from France. Ready-mades were available in American retail stores and tailor shops long before the Civil War. After 1865, we strove to inflict on ourselves and our young some of history's most tortured creations, such as the infamous Lord Fauntleroy suit, of which the museum has a pristine example, as well as a similar velvet knickerbocker suit with Zouave jacket. We can only sigh in pity for the poor ten-year-old forced into such attire, which was doubtless enhanced by the so-called "American blouse," an orgy of lace, white cotton, and oversized collar.

Female fashion of Scarlett O'Hara's time required undergirding by a collapsible crinoline cage, a cone of some thirty watch-spring steel rings growing concentrically to the floor. By the 1880s, the exuberant bouncing bell of the hoop skirt was restricted to a parabola, outlined by an all-new crinoline cage closely embracing the ankles. Soon the demands of a fuller drape required bustles, of which the museum owns a variety. Designers rushed to patent these beauty aids, formed of cotton-covered wire, and resembling fragments ripped from the viscera of upholstered chairs. The first synthetic plastic material, celluloid, was mastered by the early 1870s and sent forth masquerading as coral, jet, horn, tortoise shell, and malachite jewelry. Celluloid combs and collars were major contributors to dapper grooming in the later years of the century.

The need to clean up residential dirt was a problem made to order for the inventive spirit of the 1850s. The first carpet sweeper in America whirred out of Boston in 1858; a national magazine's enthusiastic product test report predicted the end of brooms. The museum's collection of such products begins with an 1859 Daboll, made in Providence, Rhode Island. Rolling on wheels that spun a revolving brush, the Daboll was reasonably effective. The Bissell arrived in the 1870s, boasting the improvement of an adjustable brush, as displayed in the museum's 1876 model. The Bissell would dominate the carpet sweeper market for generations.

The vacuum cleaner began late in the nineteenth century with clumsy, hand-pumped devices that required two operators. But with the rapid development of small, high-speed electrical motors, the vacuum sweeper was an obvious application, and with the advent of the first highly success-

Opposite. This Lord Fauntleroy suit of c. 1885 is probably American made. Its pants and jacket are velveteen; the blouse is linen

ful Hoover of 1908, the age of modern housecleaning had truly arrived.

The museum's collection of household laundry equipment traces the long and homely cavalcade that tried, often unsuccessfully, to ease washday drudgery. A selection of gadgets sought to improve the ancient washboard with arms and cranks. Other washers pounded, squished, and sucked. Cradle-shaped rockers like the 1876 Pennsylvanian and the Boss of 1888 made some insubstantial headway.

Kerosene was important in the home, yet its period of dominance was surprisingly short. The kerosene lamp developed only from the 1850s, when it was already plain to many scientists that electric lighting was only a matter of time. Gaslight, in use in selected locations since the beginning of the century, was a formidable rival to both kerosene and electricity. In 1885, gas was rejuvenated by the development of the Welsbach mantle, an impregnated gauze device that created a brilliant, efficient, and economical light that remained popular until 1910.

The museum's collection of lighting devices, best in the world, includes every type of light used in North America from the earliest settlers' crude imports onward, covering such rare offshoots as political parade torches, and rows of glittering chandeliers, crude wrought-iron grease lamps, stately Sandwich glass kerosene fixtures, classical Argands. An assembly of hundreds of lightbulbs traces the progression of Edison and his competitors.

In music, the upright piano had its origins as far back as the 1820s, but the popular square held the stage until after the Civil War. Then the upright age broke with full force. Here was a style that approached the grand in volume, yet would fit against the wall of all but the tiniest parlors. The upright's practicality did not inhibit its manufacturers from scaling new heights of ornamentation. The rosewood case of the museum's 1884 Baltimore-made Knabe is lavishly inlaid with maple and mahogany festoons and flowers. Inside, the sturdy iron frame had capacity to spare for the modern standard of eighty-eight notes. Knabe is also represented by a mighty rosewood concert grand, c. 1870.

*t*he mastery of new equipment by furniture factories opened the door to increasingly intricate constructions at ever-falling prices. Such styles as Rococo revival were dictated by inventive leaders like John Henry Belter of New York, whose techniques in laminating and carving were widely imitated. The Renaissance revival school employed fewer curves, but ponderous dimensions. The museum displays one Renaissance revival etagère and pier table combination, c. 1870, bristling with female heads, scrolls, swans, tassels, plaques, and swags, combining walnut, ebonized wood, gilt, and porcelain. Almost nine feet tall, this prodigy has no practical function other than serving as a mirror and resting place for three pieces of sculpture. But it does do more: such a piece sums up, as no written history

Opposite. Mighty were the works of America's mid-nineteenth-century piano craftsmen. The grand piano in the foreground came from the Baltimore shop of William Knabe & Company in about 1870. A decade before, the Kroeger Piano Company of Stamford, Connecticut, had created the harp piano, at rear

could, the tortured complexities of the Gilded Age.

A reaction did come against such monstrous (although well-made) pieces, and especially against their imitators, whose production capacity may have exceeded their quality standards. English designer Charles Eastlake was one who sought, in the 1870s, to curb design excesses, advocating plainer rectilinear forms with simple, lightly routed line carving and contrasting colors of wood. Mass producers immediately seized Eastlake's ideas and used them to create more distortions. The museum displays an Eastlake-style icebox.

A far simpler theme was the Mission style of oak furniture arriving in the 1890s. Its clean, cagelike simplicity must have struck proper late Victorians with some surprise. But it did not succeed in holding back the flood of turn-of-the-century "golden oak" furniture, disparaged in some recent decades as the nadir of American furniture design.

Historical associations fix an extra dimension of interest to such museum furniture as the massive chair and desk made in 1857 for the U.S. House of Representatives and designed by Thomas U. Walter. One of the nation's foremost architects, Walter spanned Greek revival to Romanesque revival in his long career, and was architect of the U.S. Capitol from 1851 to 1865. He enlarged the Capitol to essentially its present form, and replaced the lower Bulfinch dome with the one we see today. As part of designing the new Senate and House wings, he created new furniture as well. The deeply carved oak chairs, made by the New York firm of Bembe & Kemmel, were judged too heavy by the Congressmen, and in only two years were auctioned off and replaced. An identical chair found its way to the Washington photographic studios of Mathew B. Brady and Alexander Gardner, and was used to pose such figures as Abraham Lincoln.

President Lincoln was sitting in another chair, however, on April 14, 1865, at Ford's Theater. Today the walnut, Rococo revival rocking chair in which he was assassinated is one of the museum's supreme treasures, albeit a melancholy one. The original faded red upholstery is threadbare but intact. The left runner shows an old break at the rear. As a scar of use it is especially provocative: was the wood broken in that mad, trampling scene in the Presidential box, moments after Booth triggered his Deringer? Impounded by Secretary of State Edwin Stanton, the chair was stored for sixty-five years before returning to its owning family, and thence coming to the museum. The old rocker is made even more meaningful by two other original relics displayed across it: the drab, light brown shawl Lincoln was using, and the most fragile witness to murder, his theatrical playbill.

Persevering against the lingering American preference for foreign china, our ceramic manufacturers by mid-century were creating not only tableware but also such works of art as the museum's Parian eagle vase of 1850. It was made by the U.S. Pottery Co. of Bennington, Vermont, using a technique that imitated marble. James Carr of the New York City Pottery Co. used the medium with stunning success in 1876 with his bust of George Washington in a Roman toga. The work was exhibited at the Philadelphia Centennial, attracting great attention, just as it remains a popular museum artifact today. Similarly, a pair of vases by Thomas C. Smith & Son of New York are veterans of the Centennial. They patriotically display selected scenes and emblems of America around the base.

Such performances at the 1876 exposition helped American ceramicists become solidly established at last. That significance was lost on Mrs. Rutherford B. Hayes, who ordered a new set of Presidential china in 1878—from France. The Hayes china was, at least, decorated by an American with all-American scenes. Representative pieces join the museum's many other examples of Presidential porcelain. (It would not be until the administration of Woodrow Wilson that the White House received American-made china, from Lenox, Inc., of Trenton, New Jersey.)

Toward the close of the nineteenth century, a reaction to the uniformity of mass production inspired a new spirit of individual craftsmanship in ceramics and glass. About 1886, the Greenwood Pottery of Trenton, New Jersey, produced an artistic porcelain ewer. Ten inches tall and covered with a deep royal blue glaze and assorted gilded decorations, the ewer has an oriental look that recalls the fresh interest in Eastern design in the 1880s. Similarly, a twenty-six-inch vase made by Joseph Lycett of New York City in 1889 is elaborately ornamented with aquatic flowers, and bracketed by dolphin handles. Called the "Barber Vase," for a former owner, it is one of the museum's most important examples of late nineteenth-century ceramics. A still more personalized artistry sprang from such female artisans as Kate B. Sears, whose 1891 Parian porcelain vase displays a frieze of cupids on flying geese and the forms of stylized leaves.

By 1900, advanced artists had clearly left the old century's forms behind. The twentieth-century idea arrived on the iridescent glass wings of Louis Comfort Tiffany; that master's three-handled, blown amber vase with its irregular veining seems the very essence of Art Nouveau.

Before the Civil War most American toys were imported, but Yankee ingenuity did produce at least one antebellum breakthrough: the first modern board game. Brainchild of Anne Abbott, the daughter of a New England clergyman, the game "Mansion of Happiness" carried its players along a themed journey, through board spaces dictated by the spin of an indicator. The game fitted the time's morality. Players landing on Cruelty were sent back to Justice; a stop on Idleness would lead to Poverty; a Sabbath Breaker would be jailed and then lose three turns. But advancing to such frames as Piety, Honesty, Humility, and Industry sent the player farther along the road to the Mansion of Happiness. It was a good game and intensely popular. W. & S. B. Ives of Salem, Massachusetts, brought it out in 1843; later in the century it was marketed by Parker Brothers.

Other board games followed swiftly. The first big competitor was an 1844

Opposite. Forever haunting our history, this is the rocking chair in which President Abraham Lincoln was sitting at the moment of his assassination. He was also using the shawl and theatrical program draped on the chair. The stovepipe hat, while of the appropriate period, has no Lincoln connection

Above. This important earthenware vase was made in 1889 by the Faience Manufacturing Company of Greenpoint, New York, and decorated by Joseph Lycett. It is sometimes called the "Barber Vase" after its original owner

effort by L. I. Cohen & Co. of Philadelphia, entitled "The National Game of the Star Spangled Banner or Geographical & Historical Tourist through the United States & Canada," unsurprisingly known as the "National Game Tourist." The museum has both rare original games in its toy collection.

By the 1860s, American industry had geared up for an avalanche of iron and mechanical toys. One of the first known mass-produced wind-up toys is a ten-inch-long locomotive, made of tin with cast-iron wheels. The brightly painted engine has "Union" stenciled on the boiler. Toy aficionados praise another odd-looking toy in the museum, a spring-operated, foot-high walking doll that pushes a cartlike conveyance. In the cart a boy waves an American flag, and the whole ensemble is preceded by a dangling brass bell. An elaborate wind-up toy of the era is a fifteen-inch-long sidewheeler, two-stacked steamboat. Others—some of the best in design and detail—are unmechanized iron pull toys, like a nineteen-inch steam fire engine, with detachable driver holding the reins to a galloping team. Nearby is a lion with a bobbing head, and a Jack-in-the-Box. Such are a few of the faded toys of the Gilded Age.

The museum's collection of mechanical banks is displayed with the toys. In some cases we can see why, as with the Artillery Mechanical Bank of c. 1877. It displays a soldier aiming a mortar, which shoots a coin into a blockhouse or fort. The American Eagle Bank of 1883 features a mother eagle feeding two babies in their nest. The mother bends forward, flaps her wings, and drops a coin from her beak into the nest. Originally, this deluxe savings aid even made a chirping sound from a built-in bellows. Other popular banks were made in the form of the real thing. In one, the Magic Bank of 1876, a cashier at his post inside the building rotates and deposits the tendered coin.

*i*n the 1850s a few daredevils such as John Wise revived the nation's interest in ballooning. Wise electrified county fairs by dropping animals overboard in parachutes, and sometimes leaping out himself. Wise carried America's first official airmail two years before the Civil War. His contemporary, Thaddeus Lowe, sent down the first aerial communication (by telegraph) and founded the U.S. Army Aeronautics Corps.

Throughout the nineteenth century, dreamers tinkered with flight. England's Sir George Cayley (1773–1857) articulated some surprisingly advanced aeronautical theories, and built a successful man-carrying glider. William Henson, another Englishman, patented an aerial "steam carriage" that incorporated most of the features of an airplane. In 1848, a model of it actually flew. The first successful dirigible—designed, built, and flown by Frenchman Henri Giffard—plowed through the Paris skies at five miles per

hour in 1852. Driven by a light steam engine, the craft covered seventeen miles in a pioneering powered, manned flight. In the next generation, German Otto Lilienthal made more than two thousand glider flights before a final, fatal glide in 1896. In 1884, a nine-horsepower battery-operated electric motor drove an airship, *La France*, on a successful flight with a two-man crew of French army officers.

Apart from a few such stirring exploits, the century was firmly footed on the ground, with the railroad its chief obsession. The peak of the woodburning era, 1855 to 1875, produced the most beautiful locomotives ever built, works of industrial sculpture caparisoned with gleaming brass and brilliant painted flourishes. One of the best survivors is the museum's 1858 Rogers, representing the 4-4-0 "American" class locomotive that is one of the milestones of mechanical design. Built originally for the Atlantic & Gulf Railroad of Georgia, its name was *Satilla*. Henry Ford acquired and restored the engine in 1924, and renamed it *Sam Hill*, after an engineer who worked the Dearborn run on the Michigan Central when Ford was a boy. In 1929, when President Herbert Hoover attended the Golden Jubilee of Light that officially dedicated the museum and Greenfield Village, Ford renamed the locomotive *The President*. Meanwhile his shops had constructed three replica coaches suggesting the Civil War era, directed by Thomas Edison himself, who had worked on just such a train.

The museum's railroad section traces the entire progression of motive power through the 1880s, when the harbingers of a new era of more powerful coal burners arrived. By the late 1890s, America's main-line locomotives dwarfed the few remaining "teakettles," as they were scornfully dismissed, of the earlier era. Their increased speed and weight would not have been sustainable, however, without two basic technological improvements: the airbrake and the automatic coupler.

Before George Westinghouse invented and successfully demonstrated the airbrake in 1868, stopping a train was a crude and often dangerous process, requiring brakemen to leap from car to car, cranking down on each one's heavy brake wheel, mechanically forcing shoes against wheels with little more sophistication than the system on a Concord coach. Westinghouse, a New York-born Civil War veteran and brilliant engineer, made a technological leap in providing, in effect, the first "power brake." Compressed air, pumped by an accessory on the locomotive, was piped from car to car along the train, actuating all brakes simultaneously when the engineer pulled one lever. The new system did not eliminate train wrecks—a train would always be difficult to stop—but it was a quantum leap in train safety.

About the time the airbrake was coming into general use, in the early 1880s, E. H. Janney's automatic coupler was introduced to further applause among battered trainmen. "Coupling up" had been one of the most dangerous jobs in industry, requiring a man to stand between mating cars to guide a large link from coupler to coupler, then drop in a securing pin at the

Opposite. By the late 1850s, American locomotives had reached a high point in industrial design, as demonstrated by the museum's 1858 Rogers. This lovely woodburner was made in Paterson, New Jersey, and cost the Atlantic & Gulf Railroad $8,200 on delivery. Renamed *The President* by Henry Ford, it ceremoniously pulled President Herbert Hoover and other dignitaries to the 1929 opening of the Ford Museum and Greenfield Village

instant of impact. The process took a heavy toll in fingers and hands. But the new "knuckle"-style coupler was much safer. Both devices are demonstrated on a Baldwin passenger locomotive of the 1890s, an engine exactly twice the weight of the little 1858 woodburner, although retaining the same 4-4-0 wheel configuration. Baldwins were always in the forefront of American locomotive design. The Philadelphia company was founded by early industrialist and philanthropist Matthias W. Baldwin with the locomotive *Old Ironsides* in 1832.

Generations of our ancestors found streetcars indispensable, and Henry Ford gathered up a representative collection for his museum. The eldest is a horse-drawn car of 1881, which was approaching the end of the animal-power era. The sixteen-passenger vehicle was built by one of the leading specialists, J. M. Jones & Co. of West Troy, New York, a firm that sold thousands of horsecars around the world, including a stunning order of two hundred for Bombay, India, in 1870. The company had learned early to feel at home in shipping its vehicles across oceans; after starting in 1839 as a carriage and wagon maker, it shipped thousands of wagons around Cape Horn to San Francisco during the California Gold Rush.

The 1881 car is toylike, topheavy, and probes the upper limits of Gothic quaintness. Once it served in Brooklyn, New York; lettering still proclaims GREENPOINT, FERRIES, HUNTERS POINT & ERIE BASIN. The lettering, paint trim, ironwork, interior seating, and "Rules for Passengers" sign all combine in a priceless time capsule of American street transportation more than a century ago.

When electrical pioneer Frank Sprague created America's premier electrified street rail system for Richmond, Virginia, in 1889, the career of animal-powered cars came to an abrupt halt. The 1890s marked the end of horsecars. That any survived (the museum has two out of a national handful) is remarkable.

The replacement is epitomized by several electrics, the first an 1892 vehicle from Philadelphia's J. G. Brill Company. Anyone tempted to doubt the Victorians' quality standards should note that much of the car's trim was mahogany. Later generations of Brills are represented by the company's "Birney" class, built from 1916 into the '20s, and famed for its melodramatically named "dead man" controls. Such cars stopped automatically if the motorman's hand pulled away for any reason. That comforted the riders and allowed the trolley companies to introduce one-man service, cutting down on overhead and taking some of the pressure off an overtaxed civilian labor pool during World War I.

Commercial wagons were rarely preserved when their working lives were done, and the survival of those in the museum's collection opens an elusive window on vanished routines and technologies. An 1870 butcher's wagon recalls the time when perishable foods were sold daily in the street, or delivered door-to-door. A 1900 beer wagon once delivered kegs to pre-Prohibition saloons. One 1885 freight wagon still bears the name of the original owner, F. L. Hatch, who hauled new shoes from Massachusetts factories. Another rarity is the dump wagon of 1900, with its pedal-actuated dumping door for dispensing gravel or sand. An oil tank wagon of 1892, still emblazoned "Standard Oil Company" and "Perfection Kerosene," had compartments for gasoline and motor oil as well. A two-horse team pulled the heavy rig, whose driver enjoyed the relative comfort of a buggy top. The Standard Oil Company alone operated more than six thousand wagons at the turn of the twentieth century.

The lovely 1797 chariot already discussed was a product of the bench craftsman's golden age, and may be viewed against the same measurements of skill and technology that we apply to a bombé Chippendale chest-on-chest, a flintlock long rifle, or a hand-hammered silver coffeepot. In the century that followed, technological changes came, though at a rather slow pace at first, to the manufacture of horse-drawn conveyances. The big news came in such minor milestones as the invention of the elliptical spring early in the 1800s, and later improvements in hub construction. Gradually, with improvements in carriage suspension, manufacturers learned to make lighter vehicles that could stand the shocks of wretched roads.

Our most important vehicle of the century was the buggy. Though established in essential form before the Civil War, it was in Cincinnati in the 1870s that the type was first made with interchangeable parts. From then until about 1910, the country saw a flood of homely, practical, and unbelievably cheap buggies, averaging $35 but often discounted to $25. One of the centers of buggy and wagon manufacture was Flint, Michigan, where future automobile tycoon William C. Durant got started with the Flint Road Cart Company. The carriage makers of Flint were not merely the ancestors of the men who would make Buicks and Chevrolets—they were the same men.

Buggies were satisfactory, but not for the wealthy, who insisted on the comfort and elegance of vehicles of *grande luxe*. One maker that provided them was Brewster & Co. of New York City, which enjoyed an international reputation by the time of the Civil War. The museum displays a selection of Brewsters that span many years. An 1865 closed coach with facing seats, certainly the Rolls-Royce of its day, cost about $1,500. Less stately but still formal, a Brewster George IV phaeton was a popular type among aristocratic mid-Victorian women, who found its low profile an admirable showcase in which to display their costumes on rides through the park. The style led quickly to the Victoria, one of the most graceful vehicles ever made. The museum's example of c. 1875 has swooping leather fenders, ornately tufted upholstery, and a dark green tonneau, all slung lithesomely within four C-shaped springs. The Victoria's design—a low, rakish profile with a calash top—was so good it was transmitted to at least the early generations of American cars; the Peerless Victoria of 1911 motorized the profile for one of

J.M. Jones & Company of West Troy, New York, a preeminent producer of horse-drawn streetcars, made this charming example in 1881. It served nearly twenty years on the streets of Brooklyn, New York

the best-looking cars in this or any other museum collection.

Somehow, the excesses of design in furniture, architecture, and dress of the high Victorian era never reached the artifacts of transportation. As if guided by unerring gyroscopes of taste, carriage makers plied their trade with restraint and an increasingly sure sense of line. There seems to have been little demand for anything else. When the governor of Nevada ordered a new carriage in the raucous silver-boom year of 1870, he received a slender, sedate barouche from the maker, E. M. Miller of Quincy, Illinois. But Mr. Miller did make some concessions at the governor's request: door handles, other mountings, and harness for a four-horse team were solid silver.

Among the nicer nineteenth-century forms that vanished utterly with the coming of motorcars was the hansom cab. Designed by an English architect, the low-slung, two-wheeled, two-passenger, front-opening hansom was one of the snuggest vehicles ever devised. Curiously, Americans resisted it until late in the horse-drawn era; by the time we recognized its value, its time was almost gone. The museum's rare example is by C. P. Kimball & Company of Chicago, and dates about 1885.

The era of horsepowered vehicles drew to a close with a corresponding surge of popularity in sport coaching. Some of the finest examples of the carriage maker's skill date from the late nineteenth and early twentieth centuries. The museum's brougham of 1902, however, is of a mainline, non-sporting style favored since before the Civil War by nabobs and cab-owners alike, a practical, comfortable, low-slung carriage of elegance and strength. The style of its body was appropriated by automobile makers for almost all early coupes; as late as 1923, Ford was still making a Model T with essentially the same passenger compartment. But the most interesting thing about this brougham is its history. It was the presidential vehicle of President Theodore Roosevelt, used for official occasions throughout his administration, and on many occasions by his successors, even after President William Howard Taft motorized the White House fleet. The brougham remained in White House service until 1928.

America's most famous horse-drawn fire steamers came from Manchester, New Hampshire, where in 1859 the Amoskeag Manufacturing Co. built its first. The firm was acquired in 1877 by the Manchester Locomotive Works, which continued making horse-drawn Amoskeag steamers until 1908, for a total of 839. The museum's example, serial number 809, came in 1906, near the era's close, and is a worthy representative of the twilight years of steamers. Was there ever a creature of the American road as formidable as this great, smoke-belching machine, storming out of its firehouse behind a three-horse team? The splendid Amoskeag served in Detroit's Engine Company Number One, where it was called "Big Mike." All by itself, the pumper constitutes a textbook in American industrial design at the turn of the twentieth century.

a few early Victorian inventors fiddled with systems to add power to that humiliated protobicycle, the hobby horse. A Scot produced a lever-drive device in 1839. A true breakthrough occurred in the 1860s, when two Frenchmen applied a simple crank with pedals to the front axle. One of the inventors, Pierre Lallement, moved to Connecticut and built and patented the first American velocipede, or "boneshaker," in 1866. The firm of Pickering and Davis of New York soon made them under Lallement's patent. The museum's beautifully crafted example dates about 1870. It received very little use; by 1871, many communities had banned boneshakers as public nuisances.

Strangely, the boneshakers of the 1860s—even with their wood spokes and iron tires—have a slightly more modern look about them than the bizarre creations that came next. Back in England, even as the funeral rites of boneshakers progressed, James Starley produced the first highwheeler, or "ordinary." The odd-looking highwheeler was based on a useful mechanical principle: the larger the wheel where power is directly applied by a crank, the farther and faster the device will go with each foot-powered revolution. The practical limit to the principle was the length of the rider's legs. As manufacturers went to the maximum, wheels of sixty inches rolled majestically forth after 1878. By the early 1880s, technological progress brought many similarities to modern bicycles: wire spokes, lightweight frames, pedal construction. Yet the gigantic front wheel, tiny rear wheel, and solid rubber tires were overpowering features.

Of the museum's number of ordinaries, none is more significant than an 1884 Expert Columbia. It is like the vehicle that dashing adventurer Thomas Stevens pedaled around the world from 1884 through 1887. To be sure, he also rode and pushed for much of the way; by all odds, a heroic, 13,500-mile odyssey. The manufacturer of Stevens's bike was the formidable Colonel Albert Pope, who was also a major lobbying force for good roads and cyclists' rights. Cyclists' rights? Indeed. With the sudden bike boom, some roadside property owners became toll gougers, fleecing the generally affluent, sporting bikers. Teamsters, claiming the bikes scared their animals, shoved sticks into the highwheelers' spokes. The bikers organized the League of American Wheelmen and pushed for better roads, signs, and maps; they sanctioned races and rallies, dressed in distinctive uniforms, and built motel-like clubhouses. With bikes costing $150 each, it was a game for well-to-do adventurers. Downhill speeds of 30 m.p.h. were attainable, and outings traditionally covered 100 miles per day, no mean feat on the available roads. Such riding was dangerous, for the highwheeler had a depressing tendency to pivot forward on confronting a serious obstruction, pitching the driver straight over and down on his head. American ingenuity could produce only one major change during the perilous 1880s: switching the big wheel to the rear. Then the rider could pitch *backward*.

Opposite. The rakish, low-slung grace of the Victoria perfectly suited the style-conscious cynosures of America's Gilded Age. This fine example came from the shop of Brewster & Company of New York City, sometime around 1875

In 1885, the English technical wizard James Starley, inventor of the high-wheeler, decided its time had come. He applied a chain and sprocket drive system on a bicycle of two equal wheels called the Rover, and began popularizing a new era of "safeties." The bikes of today all had their clear beginning in Starley's Rover. Yet the shift was not immediate, for many dashing wheelmen took reckless pride in their all-male hobby, and resisted the namby-pamby influence of low-wheeled safeties. Women had begun taking to English-import tricycles, on which the rider sat between two majestic rear wheels. In about five years, however, all that was passé, and both men and women turned in droves to the new bikes. When Colonel Pope began producing the Columbia Veloce safety in 1888, the stage was set for the biking phenomenon of the 1890s. Irish veterinarian John Dunlop provided the final necessary modernization, the pneumatic tire, in 1888.

Suddenly a new social structure developed around biking. Young women now possessed a degree of individual freedom of mobility that only the most dashing horsewomen had known before. Fashion and etiquette arbiters struggled to cope. Conservative ministers warned against the dangers of unchaperoned young people loose on the roads. But most Americans accepted the bicycling craze of the 1890s as a happy, healthy social phenomenon, while the decade spawned at least 190 popular songs about bicycling. The museum's 1889 Columbia is a good example of the machine that so heavily influenced those golden years.

The biking rage and its potential for commercial riches opened the era of consumer marketing in transportation. Manufacturers cultivated bike races as sure-fire attention-getters. Such star riders as young Barney Oldfield staged challenge races, paced by four-man teams. The publicity-conscious Waltham Manufacturing Co., maker of the popular Orient line, created a famous ten-man bicycle that was demonstrated at races. The historic, if grotesque, old "Oriten" is today one of the museum's most popular bicycle exhibits. Another is the powder blue 1900 Tribune Blue Streak once owned and raced by Barney Oldfield. A similar Tribune carried Charles "Mile-a-Minute" Murphy on a historic 1899 ride in which he slipstreamed behind a speeding train to become the first human to pedal a mile in less than one minute.

*a*few pioneers—spiritual descendants of the great Oliver Evans, the steam originator, or stirred by the short-lived success of British road steamers—tinkered with steam for highway power in the middle nineteenth century. Among the most successful, early self-propelled motor vehicles in the country was the one built by Sylvester Hayward Roper of Roxbury, Massachusetts. Roper built his first car in 1863, the year that Henry Ford was born; his leisurely production schedule extended until 1896—and totaled ten vehicles. The museum's Roper, acquired by Henry Ford personally, dates

Left. An early promotional dream machine, the ten-man Oriten of 1896 drew attention to the excellent Orient "safety" bikes of Waltham, Massachusetts

Above. This 1865 Roper steam carriage is the oldest motor vehicle in the museum's collection. Sylvester Roper of Roxbury, Massachusetts, built his first steamer in 1863; his last in 1895. The charcoal-fueled Roper was acquired by Henry Ford in 1930

from 1865, and is probably America's oldest original operable motor vehicle. The Roper is a clean-looking car of the buggy style, appearing far more agile than some famous marques of later decades. A two-cylinder charcoalburner, the brakeless Roper was stopped by engaging reverse or by throttling down. Alas, the sturdy little unit was viewed by both the public and its owners as more wonderful curiosity than potentially valuable means of transportation. The original owner of the museum's model, W. W. Austin, exhibited the car at county fairs in New England and the Midwest, challenging crack trotting horses to a race. Austin and the Roper usually won. A broadside of the time claimed the car, carrying two people, could be driven 150 miles per day "upon common roads." A charge of twenty-five cents was imposed to view "the most wonderful invention of modern times."

Considering the public's long exposure to the Roper as it successfully challenged the nation's best horseflesh, it is hard to explain the car's lack of significant impact. That it was a steamer, trailing wisps of smoke from its underslung exhaust, should not have been a major objection—after all, the time was steam's heyday. The power source was accepted fatalistically by the public. A few years later, in the 1890s, a veritable fleet of steam cars appeared, and one marque—the Doble—endured into the 1930s. Still, the idea of bouncing along on a boiler of live steam did produce some squeamishness. Boilers did explode, and they were expensive to build and complicated to operate. The power source that would drive the world's automobiles was announced from Germany in 1876: Nickolaus August Otto's four-cycle, internal combustion engine. Despite all the improvements made in more than a century, Otto's principle would remain intact, unchanged in every four-stroke engine in the world—the sequence known to every mechanic as intake, compression, power, and exhaust.

The argument over who invented the automobile has been defused by a growing awareness that it is a moot question. Scant doubt remains, however, that in the annals of internal combustion, Germany's Karl Benz was first off the mark in 1885 with a workable car. Moreover, he was the first to produce a quantity of cars for public sale, building sixty-nine vehicles between 1885 and 1893. The museum's surpassingly rare 1893 Benz Velocipede represents the world's first production car. The Velo, as its devotees called it, incorporated some very modern-sounding mechanical systems for its time, including a carburetor, a gearbox, a differential, and water cooling. Apart from those features, it resembles an ungainly carriage; wonderfully original and archaic looking, the Benz seems to have sprung from an ancient tomb, and bears as much superficial resemblance to the components of modern transportation as the funeral boat of Thutmose III. Yet the Velo was a sensation. Add to its other firsts that the gawky Benz instantly gripped the international market, exporting two-thirds of its production. Years later Benz would link up with fellow-German pioneer Gottlieb Daimler, and their company prospers today. Many others made a variety of contributions in the earliest years. An eccentric Austrian named Siegfried Marcus tinkered promisingly, shunted to other projects, and was almost forgotten. American George B. Selden applied for patents on gasoline-powered cars as early as 1877 and, while never marketing a car, profited under royalties from a variety of manufacturers until defeated in court by Henry Ford.

The birth of motorcycles was nearly simultaneous with that of cars. A French "boneshaker" manufacturer, Ernest Michaux, clapped a little steam engine to one of his products in 1867. American Sylvester Roper also made a pufferbelly motorcycle. But steam was simply the wrong power source for two-wheelers, and when Gottlieb Daimler successfully applied a gasoline engine to a bike frame, the die was cast. Daimler moved on to automobiles,

leaving it to a small group of engineers in Munich to produce the world's first production motorcycle. They began experimenting in 1892, and in just two years the new Hildebrand & Wolfmuller Company was manufacturing an open-frame two-wheeler of a conformation that hardly seems out of place today, almost a century later. Studying the museum's H&W, it seems remarkable indeed that such a machine was contemporary with the first modern bicycles, and half a decade after the heyday of highwheelers. A two-cylinder, four-stroke engine with jump-spark ignition drove the cycle at a respectable twenty-four miles per hour.

The magic year for the American automobile industry was 1896, when the Duryea Brothers marketed the first production model of an American car. Originally from Illinois, Charles and J. Frank Duryea ran a bicycle plant in Springfield, Massachusetts. They successfully tested their first car in 1893, and built another in 1895. With Frank at the tiller, that car won America's first automobile race, sponsored by the *Chicago Times-Herald*. He traveled the fifty-five-mile affair at an average of seven miles per hour. Organizing the Duryea Motor Wagon Company, the brothers launched production of cars to retail for $1,500. The museum's example is the third of thirteen identical vehicles, and is apparently the only survivor. The little Duryea has an appealing look of clean, jaunty simplicity, a quality that often distinguishes the buggy-based American cars of the late nineteenth century.

Other American pioneers are well represented in the museum's vast motor vehicle collection. A tall, two-seated 1897 Haynes-Apperson recalls the saga of Elwood P. Haynes of Kokomo, Indiana, a metallurgist who in 1894 designed a car, persuaded the Apperson Brothers (Elmer and Edgar) to build it, drove it successfully, and continued making cars until 1925, believing to his grave that he had built America's first car. The Appersons went on to build splendid cars of their own, including the famous Jackrabbit.

By 1898, the year of the Spanish-American War, even a few motorized trucks were in regular service. The museum's enormous Riker of that year was electrically powered. With an empty weight of 7,550 pounds, the huge maroon truck carried a payload of two tons in its quarter-century of service for the B. Altman Company of New York. Such department stores as Altman's were among the first commercial establishments to appreciate the value of motorized transport, and reliable electrics could be used effectively for local delivery service despite their short range. The builder of the museum's historic truck, Andrew L. Riker of Brooklyn, New York, had an unusual distinction even for his technically fluid time. He manufactured motor vehicles driven by all of the three power sources—steam, gasoline, and electricity—that fought for supremacy as the nineteenth century came to its close.

Opposite. This 1896 Duryea Motor Wagon is one of thirteen identical automobiles, making it the first production car

Triumphs
of Road
and Sky

*t*he Messrs. Duryea, Haynes, Apperson, and Riker had plenty of company as they jockeyed for position in 1900, for more than sixty American manufacturers were making automobiles. Mostly the vehicles were noisy, undependable, and fragile creations that twitched feverishly when they ran at all. Such unserviceability was aggravated by the American roadway. While some city and suburban streets could adequately accommodate motorcars, the unspeakably primitive nature of the nation's rural roads seemed an overwhelming obstacle. However, such conditions offered a built-in marketing opportunity. Reliability and speed in conquering such conditions created bragging rights of the first magnitude. From the outset, manufacturers encouraged the sporting side of motoring as young bloods—deserting their bicycle clubs—bought cars and organized races, endurance runs, and hill climbs. Endurance was getting from Chicago to Milwaukee in one day. It was clear that successful long-distance journeys would shower commercial benefits on any manufacturer.

Alexander Winton of Cleveland was one of this breed, switching from bicycles to make his first car in 1897. Two years later, driving one of his own creations, Winton made a breathtaking run from Cleveland to New York in forty-seven hours, and was greeted by cheering throngs as he drove down Broadway. In 1900, he introduced a new two-seated model he called "a marvel of simplicity that can be understood by any person of average intelligence." The museum owns one of these rare Wintons, a tiller-steered, four-

Opposite. The museum has a number of cars associated with famous names and newsworthy dramas of the past, but this 1940 Chrysler parade car is in a class by itself. Used for twenty years by New York City to carry kings, war heroes, and other notables in ticker-tape parades, the Crown Imperial phaeton here carried General Dwight D. Eisenhower in a World War II victory parade. Today it serves as the official car for opening ceremonies at the annual Greenfield Village Old Car Festival

William Ford, a successful Michigan farmer, built this Dearborn Township farmhouse in 1860. Henry Ford was born here in 1863, and here, as a boy helping on the farm, he had his first encounters with machinery. As an elderly tycoon, Henry Ford finally had the house moved to Greenfield Village in 1944

passenger number with wire-spoked wheels.

Winton's glory would soon be diluted. In 1901, driving a brawny, seventy-horsepower racer against Henry Ford in a two-car event at the Detroit Driving Club, Winton took an early lead. But his engine began smoking and Ford pulled ahead to win in the car that survives today as one of the museum's rarest racing machines.

It was a crucial point in the career of young Henry Ford, just beginning his years of incomparable impact on the automotive age. Complex and enigmatic as he was, Ford comes at least partially into perspective when seen against the major events of his life.

Even the time of Henry Ford's birth was significant: July, 1863, the month of Gettysburg, one of history's great watersheds. While generals Meade and Lee pondered their next moves, Ford was born on the family farm in Dearborn, a fertile rural area just west of Detroit. The proximity to such a major, growing city stimulated the production and marketing of such profitable commodities as dairy products and hay, helping the Fords to prosper from the time young Henry's grandfather emigrated from Ireland in 1847. By 1863, William Ford, Henry's father, owned 237 acres of farmland around Dearborn, and had just completed the two-story frame home typical of those in the region, plain but not totally graceless. Henry was born in one of three upstairs bedrooms.

He soon revealed a marked mechanical aptitude, which was encouraged by his father. The boy was fascinated by watches, and soon was repairing neighbors' timepieces with tools he made himself, a telling forecast of his lifelong passion for self-reliance. On the farm, which was technologically ahead of the average, he helped maintain equipment for haying, harvesting small grains, and dairying.

For six years he attended school, a period starting at age seven that would constitute his entire formal education. Yet the boy's formative learning was surprisingly rich. Motivated strongly by teachers of high quality, he drank in the practical, positive philosophy of William Holmes McGuffey's *Readers*, and was thereby influenced toward an independent, questing life. A crushing blow came at a vulnerable age, 13, when his mother died of childbirth's complications. Henry worked on the farm full-time for three more years. In 1879, aged sixteen, he walked into Detroit and found work as an apprentice machinist, a point from which Ford's life stands as a paradigm of the stunning rapidity of change in the peak years of America's industrialization, and of the opportunities that could be wrested from that turbulent pageant. He moved quickly between mechanical jobs: building streetcars, casting iron and brass, working on steam engines. Already Detroit had become a major manufacturer of many types of machinery. The first generation of American automobile makers was in basic training.

Ford tried farming again when he married Clara Jane Bryant of Dearborn in 1888. They built a new house on forty acres bestowed by Henry's father,

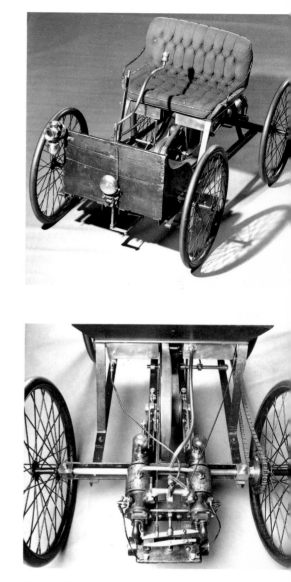

Opposite. Henry Ford himself was at the wheel of the first Ford racer, defeating Alexander Winton in a dramatic contest at the Detroit Driving Club. The man beside the mustached, intent Ford is identified as Oliver Barthel. Today, the 1901 car is in the museum's collection

Top. Working in a small shop at his Detroit home, young Henry Ford completed this little vehicle in the spring of 1896. He called it his "Quadricycle," and took it for a trial run on June 4, with a friend bicycling alongside. After tinkering with it for six months, he sold it for $200; in 1904, he bought it back for $65

Bottom. A two-cylinder, in-line, four-horsepower engine displacing 59 cubic inches was the power plant for Ford's Quadricycle

but the call of Detroit's machinery was too strong, and in 1891 they moved back to the city. Eager to study the sensational new applications of electricity, Ford began working for the Edison Illuminating Company. Nights he experimented at home, building a gasoline engine. He and Clara got it running for the first time, clamped to the kitchen sink, on Christmas Eve, 1893.

The next step was building his first car in a small brick dependency behind their Bagley Avenue home. Ford called it the "Quadricycle." We detract nothing from that historic proto-Ford by recalling that Benz, Duryea, Riker, and others were already in production. For a thirty-three-year-old self-taught mechanic, building the little car was a triumph. He used simple angle iron for the frame and wood for its skimpy body. A buggy seat of tufted fabric was mounted above the two-cylinder, in-line gasoline engine, and the entire tiller-steered production rolled on bicycle-type tires. An electric bell, mounted on the leading edge of the dashboard, warned of the vehicle's approach.

Ford failed to tailor his car to the door of his woodshed-workshop, so before the Quadricycle's first run he had to rip out the wooden frame and several bricks. Then, with a friend riding beside him on a bicycle, Ford made his first test drive on June 4, 1896. He tinkered with improvements for the next six months before selling the vehicle for $200.

Three years later Henry Ford resigned from the Edison Company, determined to build automobiles, and was personally encouraged on his course by Thomas Edison himself. In the protean year of 1899, fresh automobile companies bloomed and died almost daily in our industrial cities, and Ford's earliest venture perished with the majority. In 1901, he returned with the two-cylinder racer that defeated Alexander Winton.

Encouraged by the racing notoriety, Ford next built two ferocious-looking race cars with huge four-cylinder engines, named them "999" (after a crack New York Central locomotive) and "Arrow," and enlisted young bicycle racer Barney Oldfield as chief pilot. Dramatic photographs of the daredevil driver, clutching the two-handed tiller of 999, created an instant notoriety for Oldfield, but it was Henry Ford himself who, in 1904, drove the giant Arrow across the ice of Lake St. Clair to a new world's record for the mile, 91.37 miles per hour, etching the first American car and driver in the records of auto sport. For serious racing fans, a pilgrimage to 999 is the first stop in the museum.

Ford in 1903 created the company that continues today. The first Model A—a jaunty, successful runabout also called the "Fordmobile"—sported a steering wheel instead of a tiller. Ford quickly offered a variety of sizes and styles, testing his design and engineering ideas on the market. In 1906, he produced a large, costly tourer, the Model K, his first six-cylinder car. All the early Fords possessed a certain style, an indefinable hint of rakishness to adorn their mechanical excellence. Compared with most cars of the

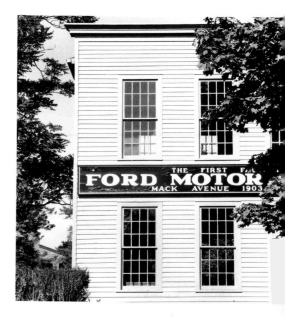

Opposite. Bicycle racer Barney Oldfield switched to cars in the dawn of auto racing, and gained still more notoriety. Here, in 1902, he grasps the steering tiller of Ford's famed "999." Ford himself raced in his early cars

Above. In 1903–04, the fledgling Ford Motor Company operated on Detroit's Mack Avenue in a building represented by this one-quarter-scale structure. The Mack Avenue operation was an assembly plant, with parts brought in and assembled at work stations. The Model T and Ford's miracles of assembly line production were years in the future

time, Fords seemed jauntier and somehow more kinetic. The lavish Model K was no exception, yet even as he made it Ford was dissatisfied, for already he was planning the work of genius that would put America on self-propelled wheels.

*b*y 1903, Alexander Winton was ready to essay the ultimate endurance trip: *coast-to-coast.* A big-bodied, two-cylinder model, equipped with one of the new steering wheels and driven by H. Nelson Jackson, churned across the continent in a race finished in sixty-three days. Winton's satisfaction was brief. Less than a month later, a much smaller one-cylinder Packard shaved two days off the Winton's time.

That was a particularly ironic blow to Alexander Winton. The Packard brothers, James Ward and William Dowd, were well-off young Ohioans who had been provoked into building cars after buying a Winton in 1898 and experiencing a fiasco of mechanical trouble. In the great race of 1903, their twelve-horsepower, 2,200-pound maroon roadster was driven from San Francisco to New York by Packard shop foreman Tom Fetch, relieved by Marius Krarup. They sensibly packed such accessories as logging chain and pick and shovel, because in places they had to make their own road. The two-month saga of Old Pacific, as the car was named, launched the Packard Company on its long and distinguished career. Today the original Old Pacific is one of the rarest relics in the museum.

America's turn-of-the-century car manufacturers accounted for less than seven thousand automobiles in 1900, year of the first auto show in the United States. Of the exhibitors in the great event, held in New York's Madison Square Garden, not one survives as a car maker, although at least two continue in altered lines. Oldsmobile was around, but didn't make the show.

Young Ransom E. Olds of Lansing, Michigan, had built steam and electric cars in the 1890s before producing his first gasoline vehicle—shaped rather like a child's wagon on enormous wheels—in 1897. He moved to Detroit, went into production, and soon stalled out with an unpopular, money-losing first edition. Olds was experimenting with several new models when a fire early in 1901 destroyed his factory, and the only thing saved was the prototype of a little one-cylinder runabout whose dashboard curved in a graceful scroll. The car was Olds's last hope. Moving back to Lansing, he produced 425 units in 1901, and 2,100 in 1902. By 1905 he had created 20,000 curved-dash models while making history as well; the Merry Oldsmobile was America's first mass-produced car. For a time Olds was selling one-third of the nation's new cars, and he beat Henry Ford to mass production by two years. The little Olds became an enduring legend as one of those rare cars to be clasped to the public bosom in universal affection—a

Opposite, clockwise from upper left. These are the Henry Ford Museum's 1903 curved dash Oldsmobile, 1912 Rauch and Lang electric town car, 1901 Columbia electric Victoria, and 1910 Stanley Steamer runabout

Above. Stately, quiet, and tractable was this 1914 Detroit Electric once owned by Mrs. Henry Ford

simple, reliable, well-made, easily controlled (and some would say cute) machine. The museum's example, a 1903 model weighing only eight hundred pounds, is a celebrated representative of America's oldest continuing car maker.

Almost a third of 1900's new models were electrics. The leader—producing about fifteen hundred—was Columbia, which had emerged from the ample organization of bicycle king Albert A. Pope in 1896. Pope would go on to make a number of marques, like Pope-Toledo and Pope-Hartford, but the museum's 1901 Columbia Electric is a rare early example of the Hartford, Connecticut, tycoon's excursion into cars. It is also unusually elegant, having been designed by an important carriage draftsman of the day, William Hooker Atwood, to follow the lines of the Victoria carriage then popular. The combination of that classic shape with the clean, silent glide of electric power created the era's ultimate car for the dignified—or timid—owner. And women felt that they needed electrics, for cranking a turn-of-the-century gasoline automobile required maximum bicep, wrist, and shoulder power.

Even after the advent of self-starters on gasoline cars, around 1912, electrics enjoyed a share of the market. Best known of some 150 companies to make them was the Anderson Electric Car Company of Detroit, whose famed "Detroit Electric" was made from 1907 to 1942. The museum owns two Detroits from the heyday of the electric car, 1912 to 1920. One is the stately black 1914 opera coupe that was once the personal car of Mrs. Henry Ford. Another popular electric is the museum's 1912 Rauch and Lang, a company demonstrating the continuity that sometimes occurred in the car business. The company had made fine horse-drawn carriages in Cleveland since 1853, and began making electrics in 1905. The 1912 town car clearly traces the Rauch and Lang heritage with its interior of pleated plush, an upholstery theme rooted in the era of luxury carriages. Mechanically superior as well, the Rauch and Lang was pushed along by its forty-one-cell Exide battery through six forward speeds, three reverse. Mourn as we may the passing of such majestic machines, their handicaps—low speed, short trip span between charges, excessive weight—proved in the end insuperable.

The experience of steam-powered cars roughly paralleled that of the electrics: each type had its advantages and its devotees, but each its fatal flaw. Steamers were fast, smooth, reliable, but a bit complex and expensive, prone to catching fire, and slow to work up to operating pressure. On balance, they were more flexible than electrics, but women shied away from the necessary fiddling with valves and gauges. The manufacturers that made steamers popular and practical were the Maine-born Stanley brothers, F. E. and F. O., a pair of bearded, derbied, identical twins from Newton, Massachusetts. The Stanleys, who had already succeeded in producing X-ray equipment, home gas generators, photographic dry plates, and violins, pro-

Opposite. One of the most historic cars in the Ford collection is Old Pacific, the Packard that endured a sensational, two-month, coast-to-coast dash in 1903

Opposite. The immortal Model T: while it would undergo cosmetic facelifts in the course of a nineteen-year history, the original car (exemplified by this 1909 model) remained largely unchanged

Above. Direct ancestor of today's GMC trucks and coaches, the 1906 Rapid was built by Detroit's Max Grabowsky

vided additional proof that clever inventors and tinkers could, if they set their minds to it and applied some hard-headed Yankee business sense, produce a better car. And the Stanleys made it look deceptively easy. Their first steamer, in 1897, was an immediate success, combining grace and practicality. The Stanleys, keen and decorous, followed the crowd in only one way: seeking the publicity of successful speed trials. The results were breathtaking. In 1906, race driver Fred Marriott hurtled down Ormond Beach, Florida, at 127.66 m.p.h. in a torpedo-shaped Stanley Rocket, setting a new world's record and becoming the first American car and driver to win since Henry Ford in 1904. The next year, with the racer's steam pressure raised to a prepotent 1,300 pounds (compared to the Stanley standard of 600), Marriott reached 197 m.p.h., went airborne, and crashed. Marriott was seriously injured in the ghastly mess; while he survived, the conservative Stanleys lost heart for racing. The fact that the boiler did not explode was inadvertently a publicity bonus, but the Stanley was always totally safe from steam explosions; the brothers wrapped so much piano wire around each boiler that bursting was impossible.

The museum shows two Stanleys of high interest. A 1903, eight-horsepower model demonstrates the new design of 1902 that established the Stanley's superiority over other steamers. The 1910, ten-horsepower, four-passenger Model 60 runabout is the classic steamer of American legend, its coffin-shaped hood proudly garnished by the brass script, "Stanley." Here was a smooth, fast, powerful car for the modest figure of $850. Keeping their prices down was further proof of the Stanleys' ingenuity, for they had no truck with cost-cutting mass-production methods. Painstakingly creating each car by ancient shop methods, their production—which ended in the middle 1920s—totaled only eighteen thousand. All told, the brothers were atypical ornaments of the early automobile business, even to the tragedy that darkened their final years. In 1918, F. E. heroically ditched his steamer to avoid some careless roadblockers, thus becoming the first important American car maker to die at the wheel of his own product.

Famous as it was, the Stanley did not have everything its own way in the world of steam. The chief competitor was the White, begun in 1900 by the long-successful White Sewing Machine Co. of Cleveland. Early models showed speed and reliability, and when the museum's 1902 Model A Stanhope was introduced, the company bore down on one technological advantage White had on Stanley: it would get steam up faster. "Gives pressure in five minutes," White's ad copy said. By 1907, such Whites as the museum's seven-passenger Model G touring car carried a majestic "Pullman" body on a 115-inch wheelbase, trimmed out "in the most luxurious fashion which the carriage builder's art can suggest." The high, regal White, made originally for a French customer, was clear proof that in just a decade or so of manufacture, American cars could compete with European ones in luxury and sophistication.

One of the collection's most appealing vehicles is also the historic ancestor of a long line of modern trucks and buses. Max Grabowsky, a talented Detroiter who had mastered the trades of machinist and locksmith, succumbed to the motor vehicle rage in 1901. After selling a few delivery trucks under his own name, Grabowsky switched to the *Rapid* title in 1904 and started building heavy gasoline-powered trucks as one of the very first to enter that uncertain field. When he created the museum's 1906, twelve-passenger vehicle, he called it a "tourist"—the word "bus" was not yet applied to such machines. The successful Rapid lived up to its name, for with a cruising speed of fifteen miles per hour it was twice as fast as horse-drawn vehicles, and was a particular favorite for station-to-hotel service and sightseeing. For such reasons, the Rapid—nee Grabowsky—was a logical candidate for acquisition in 1909 when William C. Durant, probably the greatest organizational genius of the automotive industry, was putting together the General Motors Corporation. The Rapid throve and grew under GM, and lives today as a world leader in trucks and buses. Grabowsky by another name is today's GMC Truck & Coach Division.

The Rapid gleams in pin-striped, showroom-new restored condition, as do many of the museum's vehicles. Others survive in original condition, and thus in varying degrees display their honest scars. That may be more evocative if less beautiful. One example is the rare 1909 American truck, made in Battle Creek, Michigan, one of the few surviving early vehicles with four-wheel drive. Despite having only two cylinders, the American could pack a heroic five-ton load in its stake body.

Plumbing manufacturer David Dunbar Buick had already earned his way into the pantheon of innovation with a process for porcelainizing bathtubs. Thereafter the challenge of the infant automobile business was too great to ignore, and Buick formed his company in 1903. His reasonably priced, sturdy car was acquired by William C. Durant, who by 1907 had pushed the company to a place in industry sales second only to Ford. The 1908 Model F in the museum collection was a good buy at $1,250; it was a straightforward car, whose side-entrance tonneau held five adults and whose two-cylinder opposed engine generated a respectable twenty-two horsepower. But the most significant thing about the museum's oldest Buick is its date, 1908, the year that Durant organized General Motors.

*U*ntil the Model T Ford burst on the scene in October 1908, cars were still toys for the well-to-do. But the new car was instantly recognized as the long-awaited auto for the multitudes, and its marvelous usefulness shone through at the unveiling. If today it appears comically high off the ground, remember that the Ford was designed to churn through quagmires and clear the high-mounded centers of dirt roads. Pivoting on ingenious front radius rods, cushioned on indestructible transverse leaf springs, and rolling on chrome-vanadium steel axles, the "T" was built to grapple with rocky trails and cruel bumps.

Advanced for its time, the engine was cast *en bloc* with four big cylinders and, wonder of wonders, a detachable head. While its twenty-two horsepower may seem small, it was impressively greater than most steam traction engines. Nothing on the car, with the possible exception of the planetary transmission, was too arcane to be grasped and repaired by any reasonably coordinated amateur. Ford's demand for simplicity meant there was little to go wrong. A magneto produced the car's electricity. A single pump dispensed oil to engine, transmission, and universal joint. Gravity fuel feed and a thermosiphon cooling system forestalled troublesome pumps. The car carried five in reasonable comfort, cruising at forty miles per hour and twenty-three miles per gallon. The back seat allowed room for a farmer's milk cans. At a price of $850, the Model T was a premier mechanical miracle.

Demand was so strong that, by 1914, Ford had launched a radically expanded production system on a scale unprecedented in manufacturing, and grafted mass production onto the principle of a moving assembly line. Ford said he got the idea from a long-established technology in the midwestern meat-packing industry, "the overhead trolley that the Chicago packers use in dressing beef." The butchers were taking things apart; Ford reversed the process and retained the basic principle of bringing the work to the worker. As a moving assembly line carried Model Ts through the plant, belt conveyors fed parts to each work station. "Mass production," Ford wrote in his usual terse prose, "is the focusing upon a manufacturing project of the principles of power, accuracy, economy, system, continuity, speed and repetition."

The man-hours required to assemble a car soon dropped to about one-tenth the former time, enabling Ford to drop prices as well. The car that retailed for $850 in 1908 would average from $300 to $600 for most of its long career. By 1925 a basic roadster without electric starting cost $260, a fully equipped "Fordor" sedan $660. For a time, more than half America's new cars were Fords. In the T's glorious eighteen-year history few mechanical changes ever came. Electric lights and optional self-starters were the main technical refinements. The bright colors of early Fords were abolished in 1914, and the brass radiator was a war material casualty in 1916.

A degree of cross-pollination marked the early automobile industry and its motley crew of machinists, engineers, tinkerers, and promotional geniuses. Henry M. Leland, a distinguished Detroit manufacturer of machine tools, was first associated with Henry Ford in about 1901. Then Leland quickly gave birth to the Cadillac, of which the museum's 1903 specimen is a rare survivor of the first production year. In 1912, Henry Leland's Cadillac sprang two genuine innovations: a standard self-starter and standard electrical lighting, first in the industry. Cadillac had won the

On the line in the Highland Park Ford plant, 1913: dropping an engine into a new Model T

167

important Sir Thomas Dewar Trophy for its mastery of parts interchangeability in 1908; it scored another of the coveted English awards for the starter, a sure sign American cars had come of age. In 1915 Leland introduced the nation's first V-type, water-cooled, eight-cylinder engine at a time when the industry standard was four cylinders.

Still not finished, Leland in 1920 created the Lincoln, a massive prestige car that he proceeded to make by such expensive methods—and with such unexciting bodies—that the venture was soon in peril. Henry Ford bought the company, retained Leland's quality, restyled the bodies, and experienced instant success on unveiling his new prestige car. In an odd tribute to those early Lincolns, they were soon favored by gangsters and police. Henry Ford also gave one to his friend Thomas Edison. That car, a green 1923 V-8 of eighty-one horsepower, is displayed in the museum today, with a photograph of Edison at the wheel.

When William Durant was fitting together the pieces of General Motors in 1909, he hired French immigrant Louis Chevrolet to drive on his Buick racing team. Durant lost control of GM almost as soon as it began (he would stage a dramatic recapturing years later) and, starting over, began manufacturing a car newly designed by Chevrolet, his name fortuitously enhanced by fame as a racer. Buyers of the first-year Chevy in 1912 found it a tough performer, and the car succeeded despite its rather dowdy profile. Some snap was added to the line in 1914 with the Royal Mail Roadster, and a companion touring car, the Baby Grand. The museum's 1915 Royal Mail is indeed a rakish sport, with an elliptical gas tank of distinctive profile slung behind the tonneau. The Royal Mail was a good value for $750.

Many high-quality cars came and went in the tumultuous early years, but for many Americans of means the choice was defined by a glib alliteration: "Packard, Pierce-Arrow, or Peerless." The Cleveland-based Peerless reigned from 1901 to 1932, invariably as expensive as it was lovely. The museum's 1911 Peerless Victoria closely resembles the best horse-drawn carriages of the transition period, and its leather-topped body was applied by Brewster & Company for a total cost of $6,250. Despite its vast dignity, Peerless was a mechanical innovator, and one of the few makers of limousines to enter endurance runs, completing a 1,500-mile struggle from New York to St. Louis in 1904.

Good as it was, somehow the Peerless never quite lodged itself in American folklore as Pierce-Arrow did. Perhaps that was because—in addition to consistently advanced engineering, top reliability, and Olympian luxury—Pierce had a gimmick: after 1913, its headlights were ostentatiously faired into its fenders. Thus in a time of bewildering automotive variety, the Pierce was so instantly recognizable that in only one year (1928) did the company stoop to affixing its name to the radiator shell. The museum shows a jewel-like 1904 P-A roadster with a fifteen-horsepower, two-cylinder engine.

Opposite, clockwise from upper left. Shown here are the Henry Ford Museum's 1911 Peerless Victoria, 1916 Packard "Twin Six," 1929 Packard speedster, and 1915 Chevrolet Royal Mail

Above. Pierce-Arrow produced its first car in 1901; the museum's 1904 "Great Arrow" looks sleek for its time

The end of the "brass era" roughly coincided with the advent of electric lights and starters after 1912, although some cars, like Fords, clung to brass radiators until World War I. Most car owners and chauffeurs rejoiced in the freedom from polishing brass, and enjoyed their reflections in the easy, durable shine of new nickel-plated fittings. With lights, starters, and styling came new engineering progress, a surge forward just before World War I.

Packard was a clear polestar among luxury cars. In 1916, Packard scored with the introduction of the twelve-cylinder Twin Six, a V-12 of superb performance and flexibility, and the first American engine to employ aluminum pistons. While its eighty-five horsepower at 3,000 revolutions per minute may seem bland today, it was sensational in 1916. A racing version, generating 240 horsepower, carried Ralph De Palma to a new land speed record. Soon, the Twin Six would evolve into World War I's famous Liberty aircraft engines, first of a long line of distinguished Packard power plants for the air. The museum's example of the Twin Six is a gigantic black 1916 touring car on a 125-inch wheelbase. The passage of almost seventy years has not diminished its force of character, revealed in a trenchant, almost brutal, mass of angles, curves, and rivets crouched behind imperious headlamps under a vast leather top. "Ask The Man Who Owns One," indeed; everyone already knew he craved a Packard. When Warren Gamaliel Harding became the first president motor-borne to his inaugural, he rode in a Packard Twin Six.

The firm's red hexagon trademark already was long established by 1916, as well as the distinctive radiator shell contour that would evolve into one of the loveliest in automotive history in Packard's aesthetic heyday, 1928–36. Such examples as the museum's 1929 tan and black speedster are among the most pleasing cars ever built, and epitomize the avidly desired "classic era."

But other choices confronted those smitten by the lust for advanced performance. Mercer and Stutz were special favorites of the bugs-on-the-teeth-and-goggles clique before the term "sports car" was even coined. Mercer, of Trenton, New Jersey, unleashed its legendary Type 35 raceabout in 1911. The Mercer's greatest rival, the Stutz Bearcat, came from Indianapolis, Indiana, in 1914. In their best days, just before World War I, both cars were brawny, stark machines that to the dismay of macho purists were toned down and refined at the dawn of the flapper age. The museum's 1923 Bearcat confirms the domestication. More grand touring machine than true sports car, the yellow and black Stutz is still a jaunty, appealing roadster, ahead of its time in style, and a favorite with museum visitors. Not far away stands a 1916 Mercer sport touring car that testifies to the marque's reputation among automotive insiders of its time. It was the honeymoon car of Mr. and Mrs. Edsel Ford.

Another speedster of formidable vigor was the Apperson Jackrabbit, of which the museum shows a six-cylinder specimen from 1916. In the 1920s a new performer arrived that would eclipse almost everything on the road.

Opposite. Hubcaps from wooden wheels of the teens and twenties recall some once familiar, but long departed, automotive names

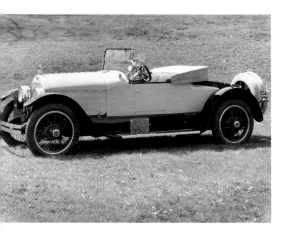

Opposite. The 1931 Duesenberg is one of today's ultimate collector cars

Above. The Stutz Bearcat of 1923 showed considerable refinements from its he-man days before World War I

The Duesenberg brothers, Fred and August, began making distinguished racing machines before World War I, and by 1920 they scored well on the sports car market with the racer-based, ninety-horsepower Model A. It carried the unusual refinement of four-wheel hydraulic brakes, pioneered by the Duesenbergs when most cars still struggled to stop with rear-only mechanical brakes. In 1926, the Indianapolis marque was obtained by financier E. L. Cord, who was already making popular and sporty Cords and Auburns in Auburn, Indiana. Cord gave the Duesenbergs carte blanche to build the biggest, fastest, most altogether noble car in America, and they responded with the wonderful Model J in 1928. A "Dusie" could accelerate from zero to 100 in seventeen seconds. Upon its monstrous, 153-inch-wheelbase chassis, America's finest custom coachbuilders—Derham, Judkins, Le Baron, Murphy—draped their best coachwork, more than doubling the $8,500 cost of a chassis alone. Though a car for millionaires, the Duesenberg managed to survive the Depression to 1937. Its last years, however, were without the uncompromising leadership of Fred Duesenberg, who in 1932 joined F. E. Stanley in that select fraternity of car makers killed driving their own product. The museum's majestic, two-and-one-half-ton Model J convertible Victoria dates from 1931.

Owning the factory led automotive pioneers to some irresistible caprices. When Walter P. Chrysler planned a new Imperial landau for his personal use in 1932, he began by decreeing an all-aluminum body for the big 146-inch wheelbase chassis, powered by a high-compression straight eight of 125 horsepower. He ordered such deluxe interior features as a bar, desk, vanity cases, and, naturally, a rear speedometer and clock. When he received the car it was blue, but Mr. Chrysler changed his mind about the color. He owned a Ming vase bearing a subtle, smoky shade of red; match *that,* he told the factory, and repaint. The result was a lovely, low-slung creation glowing like cinnamon-hued marzipan, today one of the museum's most artistically satisfying cars.

Chrysler was entitled to enjoy the fruits of his success. A veteran of the Buick and Willys organizations, he took over the Maxwell-Chalmers firm in 1923 and soon replaced those names with his own, adding a luxury line of Imperials. In 1928 he acquired the Dodge Company, launched the new marques Plymouth and De Soto, and the modern Chrysler Corporation was on its way. The Dodge had been a reliable if somewhat stodgy workhorse for years, favored for desert exploring and army use, and by prosperous farmers. The museum's 1918 Dodge touring car, uninspiring as it may seem, represents the sort of yeoman car—its fenders broad and stout enough to lug bags of fertilizer—that endeared itself to Americans more concerned with practicality than aesthetics.

In 1927, having caused enormous consternation among his dealers by shutting down his plants for six months to retool, Ford sent forth the Model A. The industry's greatest sequel was a bit overdue, as time had caught up with the wonderful Flivver—the immortal Model T—several years before.

The nation sang a popular new song, "Henry's Made a Lady Out of Lizzie," and the Model T was an overnight anachronism. But it was the quiet influence of Edsel Ford, more than Henry, that gave the Model A its excellence of design, resembling a baby Lincoln. The "A" was one of the very few basic cars available in such snappy configurations that even the wealthy did not mind occasionally being seen in one. A good example is the museum's balsam green 1928 roadster; another the 1930 phaeton.

Ford tried to give the very first one off the line, a two-door sedan, to Thomas Edison, who said thanks but he preferred open cars. Ford remade the car as a four-door phaeton, trimmed in leather. Edison accepted the revised version, which in later years was presented by Mrs. Edison to the museum, where it joins a select gathering of cars of famous personalities. One is Charles A. Lindbergh's 1928 Franklin sedan. As Lindbergh's "Spirit of St. Louis" was air-cooled, the public relations value to the air-cooled Franklin was evident, and the firm renamed one series the "Airman." J. P. Morgan's Rolls-Royce is another link with names of the past; an American body by Brewster graces the 1926 chassis.

Harvey S. Firestone ordered a massive 1929 Lincoln with convertible Victoria body by Dietrich, a leader in custom bodywork. The Firestone Lincoln reveals a Dietrich innovation: a back seat in a two-door convertible. Among many Ford family cars is Edsel's own Continental, a design created under his personal supervision.

Lincolns seemed to attract celebrities, or vice versa. The museum's rather British-looking V-12 convertible limousine was built for King George VI and Queen Elizabeth, touring the U.S. and Canada in 1939. It was dusted off again for a North American visit by Queen Elizabeth II and Prince Philip. Another 1939 Lincoln attracts a great deal more attention, however: the White House "Sunshine Special," an enormous four-door convertible crafted for President Franklin D. Roosevelt, who enjoyed riding with the top down. In 1942, security demanded its remodeling with armor plating, and bullet-proof glass, tires, and fuel tank. Bearing its five-ton weight uncomplainingly, the huge car rolled through World War II, traveling with FDR to Yalta, Casablanca, Teheran, and Malta. President Truman finally retired the Sunshine Special in 1950, and accepted a new Lincoln, which served even longer. In the Eisenhower administration, the addition of a new plastic lid over the rear bestowed its enduring nickname, "Bubbletop." The car served as a spare during the administrations of John F. Kennedy and Lyndon B. Johnson, and arrived at its final museum home in 1967. Still another presidential Lincoln is here, but unlike the other two its associations are tragic. The 1961 convertible sedan that carried President Kennedy on his final motorcade in Dallas seems to surprise visitors. "Is that really the car?" they ask. "Are you sure?" Long, black, and somehow enigmatic, the car underwent major rebuilding and armoring after Dallas, and finally was retired from White House service in 1977.

Opposite. Walter Chrysler's 1932 Imperial owes its color to a Chinese vase from the auto magnate's collection

Above. Sequels often disappoint, but not Ford's Model A, one of the best cars of all time. After almost twenty years of the Model T, the "A" was perhaps overdue; it lasted only from 1927 to 1931. But then, as years passed, such models as this 1928 roadster never really waned in popularity, and eased gradually into the status of collector's item

The development of America's networks of automotive dealerships, a necessary apparatus, was rooted in the bicycle boom of the 1890s. Local bike dealers were accustomed to franchise arrangements with such manufacturers as Pierce Arrow, Pope, Rambler, Stearns, Waverly, and White. When the factories began making cars, many bicycle agencies became car dealers overnight. Henry Ford, himself an enthusiastic biker, plucked many successful two-wheel dealerships for his fast-growing dealership chain. For the dealers it was a natural progression, and a necessary one; bikes entered a precipitous decline in popularity as the twentieth century progressed. The red-blooded bikers of the 1880s and '90s were the pioneer automobilists of the 1900s. The addition of the coaster brake in 1906 was basically the last great bicycle invention. By 1910, bicycles were for kids.

Motorcycles were something else. A Swedish-born toolmaker, Oscar Hedstrom, created the first "Indian" for the Hendee Manufacturing Co. of Springfield, Massachusetts, after only four months on the job. An instant success in the marketplace, the Indian also proved its mettle in the nation's first motorcycle endurance contest, a Boston-to-New York run in 1902. For more than fifty years, until the line's lamented passing in 1953, Indians were a daring, rakish accent on the American road. The museum shows two early specimens: a 1904 that weighs only ninety-eight pounds, and a dashing red and gold 1911 of 140 pounds.

Harley-Davidson, the last survivor of more than 150 American motorcycle manufacturers, made its debut in 1903 with a one-speed, no-clutch model that needed a push to start. Production date of the museum's first Harley, a gray and maroon entry with a squarish tank, was 1907. After World War I, our motorcycles took on essentially the profile that endures today, and some of the museum's handsomest examples are veterans of the jazz age. Charles A. Lindbergh's twin-cylinder Excelsior was delivered to him new in 1920, whereafter he used it for about five years. Similar in appearance, but more powerful with its big four-cylinder engine, the museum's big Cleveland of 1928 could better one hundred miles per hour, but the speed was insufficient to outrace the Great Depression. Cleveland failed in 1930.

The first motorized fire trucks were gasoline-powered front-wheel-drive tractors pulling existing steam pumpers. As early as 1910, however, the modern fire truck appeared, drawing both motive power and pump power from a single gasoline engine. Perhaps as a bow to the turbulent traditions of firefighting, the new equipment was more ferociously strident than necessary and would remain so. Fire trucks were so massively engineered that they never wore out but were phased out as technological refinements occurred. Many today are in the hands of private collectors. The museum shows a handsome 1928 American La France, of Elmira, New York, that remained in the city service at Wayne, Michigan, for half a century.

Opposite. Successor to the "Sunshine Special," this 1950 convertible Lincoln limousine served four United States presidents, but is chiefly remembered from the Dwight Eisenhower years when its tonneau was fitted with a plastic "bubble top"

Top. The 1939 Presidential Lincoln, dubbed the "Sunshine Special," carried Franklin D. Roosevelt through World War II. The armor-plated behemoth (9,300 pounds) even accompanied FDR to such key settings as Yalta, Casablanca, and Teheran. After the war, until 1950, the car remained in White House service under President Harry S. Truman

Bottom. Next to serve the White House as primary parade car, this 1961 Lincoln Continental was carrying President John F. Kennedy in the parade in Dallas on November 22, 1963. Extensively rebuilt thereafter, it was used by four subsequent presidents and retired in 1977

178

*t*he glamour of early 1900s motor vehicles had its counterpoint in the virility of steam railroading. By 1902, when the museum's magnificent Alco-built Schenectady passenger locomotive was built, the clear image of the twentieth century was apparent. Gone were the high, quaint, Gothic domes, the bulbous exhaust stacks, the overall balance of vertical and horizontal lines that made the older engines objects of such charm. Instead, the Schenectady is the very image of power, immensely high yet thrusting forward as if still yearning to speed out on the Detroit–Chicago run of the Michigan Central. Look at its enormous, slim-spoked drive wheels and crisply machined connecting rods; climb into its solid walnut cab and see the big dials and gauges, and all the nickel-plated trim. Imagine the Schenectady thundering through the Midwest in the year before the Wright Brothers flew. In such machines we see the start of the final phase of America's romance with the railroad.

Original coaches appropriate to the time include the private Pullman, or business car, of a Michigan railroad president. Its massively crafted oak interior, just as heavy and solid as a pre–World War I designer could possibly make it, reminds us that George Pullman himself began his career as a cabinetmaker (although Pullman was long dead before this car was made). Like Cyrus McCormick, but for different reasons, Pullman moved to Chicago, correctly perceiving that that city would be the hub of future transcontinental train travel over vast distances. He began making sleeping cars in the 1850s, and during the Civil War created the innovative luxury car with convertible berths that set the pattern for generations of "Pullmans." From 1867 on, the Pullman Palace Car Company controlled the luxury long-distance trade through the golden years of railroading. The hoi polloi traveled in less elegant circumstances, frequently in such coaches as the museum's early twentieth-century "combination" car. Very useful on small lines and local runs, it included a coach, a smoking section, and a baggage compartment.

The most recent locomotives in the collection are as dissimilar as any two machines could be, granted that each was designed for the same work. Each is, in its way, historic in the extreme. The older of the two (by fifteen years) is paradoxically the most modern, for it is the museum's only excursion into Diesel locomotive power. Homely as a rolling construction shack, the 1926 Ingersoll-Rand represents the nation's first successful Diesel locomotive. One of a series introduced in 1925, the machine was built in a cooperative venture among General Electric, the American Locomotive Company, and Ingersoll-Rand, which manufactured the Diesel engine and marketed the locomotive. Power from the six-cylinder oil burner was converted into electrical energy, used in turn by the locomotive's traction motors to produce strong, reliable, smooth motive power. It was, as engineers of the day saw the matter, a means of getting the benefits of electrical power

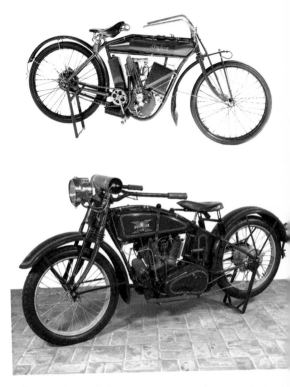

Opposite. America's first motor scooter was the Autoped of 1915. Performance was certainly respectable for its tiny, one-cylinder engine: an Autoped driver could, if he managed to keep standing, reach 35 m.p.h.

Above. Rakish mounts of our lengthening motorized past, these early cycles still suggest excitement and speed. The 1911 Indian (top) was one of a long, distinguished, and now extinct line. This one-cylinder model cost $225. Charles A. Lindbergh bought the two-cylinder Excelsior (bottom) new in 1920, and drove it for about five years. Later, he personally presented it to the museum

without all the bother of building overhead wires and transmitting electricity. They were correct in everything. The Ingersoll-Rand Diesels of the mid-1920s were so good that they remained in service for decades. The museum's example labored at the New Jersey plant of one of its parents, Ingersoll-Rand, until donated to the museum in 1970. It is original and unaltered, and thus despite its exceptional lack of charm constitutes one of the most satisfactory industrial-history artifacts of all time. Old Number 90 is a genuine pioneer.

The same cannot be said for the most recent locomotive in the museum's collection. The 1941 Chesapeake & Ohio Allegheny class coal burner is one of the largest, strongest motive power sources ever built, and in a sense one of the most beautiful. That it was one of the last only adds an ineffable sense of doomed allure to the giant "Big Al." The Lima Locomotive Works built more than sixty like it in the 1940s, all destined to haul the World War II coal of labor chieftain John L. Lewis's United Mine Workers. The Allegheny's 8,000-horsepower boiler was the largest ever built in a steam locomotive. The great engine steamed through the mountains of Virginia, West Virginia, and Kentucky with 160 loaded coal hoppers, a burden of almost ten thousand tons, at speeds between thirty and sixty miles per hour. More than sixteen feet tall and 125 feet long, the locomotive and tender weighed six hundred tons, and cost $250,000 to produce in 1941. The tender carried twenty-five tons of fuel and twenty-five thousand gallons of water. "Big Al" rolled more than four hundred thousand miles before steaming up to the museum's back door on its final run. The door, naturally, was too small, and some of the wall was dismantled before the locomotive eased to its final stop. The orange legend "C&O for Progress" still adorns the black, brutish snout of the greatest steam engine ever to thunder through the Alleghenies, and quite probably the favorite artifact of the thousands of daily visitors to Henry Ford Museum.

Ford loved steam engines and understood them perfectly, yet he sensed their ultimate shortcomings. He knew in particular that the days of steam on the farm were numbered. In 1907, he experimented with an early tractor even before launching the Model T. But other manufacturers beat Ford to the market with efficient, lightweight, gasoline-powered tractors. By 1913, it was clear the new generation of lightweight power sources would prevail. After experimenting for a decade, Ford unveiled the Fordson tractor in 1917. Like the Model T it was inexpensive, reliable, and simple, and thoughtfully designed to make life better for the masses. America's horse population plummeted as the Fordson became our most popular farm tractor. In 1925, for instance, 75 percent of all tractors made were Fordsons. By 1928, its price tag was a humble $495.

Ford had presented Fordson Number One to that genius of vegetable genetics, Luther Burbank. In later years, gathering up artifacts for his museum, the manufacturer asked for the old tractor back, and sent a new one

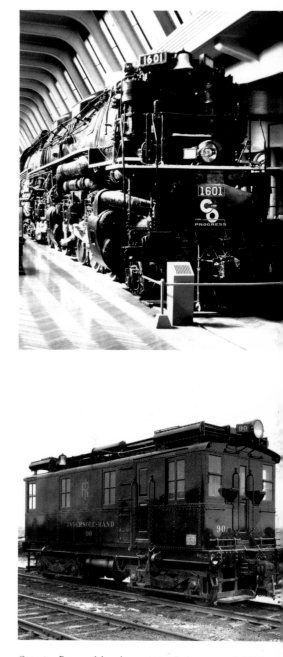

Opposite. Purposeful sculpture in steel, the museum's 1902 Schenectady locomotive rolled on 79-inch wheels. This thoroughbred steamer was built for fast passenger service by the American Locomotive Company

Top. Supreme creation of the coal-burning age, the C&O's Allegheny class locomotive generates ineffable star quality

Bottom. The museum's pioneering Ingersoll-Rand Diesel of 1926 heralded the future of rail power

to replace it. Burbank shipped the machine to Dearborn from his home in balmy Santa Rosa, California. Water-cooled vehicles like the Fordson required no antifreeze in Santa Rosa, but they did in Dearborn, and the unprotected tractor soon froze. Cracked block and all, the homely Fordson Number One is one of the most historic farm exhibits in the museum.

Experts refer to two major revolutions in American farming. The first revolution's peak years coincided with the Civil War, brought efficient mechanization to the farm, and substituted horse power for human power. That revolution, which meant that an individual could farm more land, continued through the introduction of gasoline tractors, and then culminated in 1938 with an odd-looking red and yellow device of supreme importance. The Massey-Harris combine, which pioneered self-propelled grain harvesters, eliminated the towing tractor. Highly maneuverable, frugal with fuel and manpower, and more efficient in gathering grain, the Toronto-made Massey-Harris combine was the final burst of mechanization of the first agricultural revolution. The second revolution, which is still in progress and not within the museum's purview, is the age of agricultural science, the use of hybrids, pesticides, and herbicides that has so startlingly increased production per acre.

Of even more specialized interest than such machines as the museum's Massey-Harris are exemplars of factory equipment that helped the twentieth century reach full speed. The Ingersoll milling machine of 1912, for example, stood at the heart of Ford's ability to produce the Model T so successfully. The massive device, twenty-one feet long, was used in Ford's Highland Park plant to simultaneously mill the bottoms and main bearing mounts of fifteen Model T engine blocks. Only one semiskilled operator was required to run the machine. Similarly, an Acme automatic bar machine represents the first of a kind that enabled one unskilled laborer to produce vast numbers of identical small parts.

Such machine tools were among the last belt-driven factory equipment. By the 1930s, a new generation of tools was powered by individual electric motors. One of the most significant in the museum's collection is a 1941 Bridgeport milling machine. In that streamlined apparatus, painted a now-familiar institutional gray, we see a modern landmark of the machine tool industry: a device, mass-produced itself, that made other machines. Modest in price and rugged in performance, the Bridgeport turret milling machine was no thing of beauty by orthodox artistic standards, but nevertheless was a work of art in the eyes of machinists and industrial engineers.

The museum's chronological finale tends to fall around 1950, with a few signal exceptions. One is a 1961 Unimate robot, the first ever installed on a production line. The robot spent its working career in the hot, dangerous task of unloading fresh castings and placing them in a cooling bath. Its successors would toil patiently in a myriad of assembly line jobs.

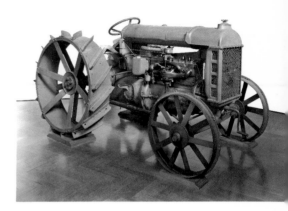

Opposite. Henry Ford (center) seemed pleased with the progress of a Fordson tractor working near Dearborn in 1919. The other men are unidentified

Above. This Fordson, production model #1, was presented to Luther Burbank by Henry Ford, who later retrieved it for his museum

183

*g*erman physicist Heinrich Hertz discovered electromagnetic radiation in 1886. Others took his laboratory experiments into the zone of practicality, and Italian Guglielmo Marconi actually transmitted Morse code for more than one mile in 1895. Inventing the first practical antenna, he patented his invention in England, where he received financial backing and started building ship-to-shore wireless systems for Morse transmissions. Among the museum's relics from the birth of radio are replicas of a Marconi receiver and transmitter of 1901, and a 1906 American-made wireless set, perhaps the first production-model receiver.

Experiments soon began with the wireless transmission of voice and music. England's John A. Fleming invented the radio-wave-detecting tube in 1904, and Lee de Forest created the three-element, or audion, tube, which amplified the waves as well. The next leg up came in 1912, with Edwin H. Armstrong's contribution of the regenerative receiver, and was followed in 1918 by his invention of the superheterodyne circuit. The right elements were in place at last and, in 1920, radio station KDKA went on the air in Pittsburgh.

Production-model receivers from the years of radio's commercial beginnings are some of the most appealing examples of American industrial design. The complete development of RCA Radiola models is traced through the 1920s. A 1924 Federal, a bristling concoction of black dials, still conjures something of the thrill that touched its first owner. The wonderful Atwater Kent Model 10, affectionately known as "the breadboard," is displayed along with several other rare, excellent specimens. Anyone who thinks craftsmanship died with the nineteenth century needs only to examine these exquisitely made radios from the late, lamented Philadelphia manufacturer.

While the battery-powered receivers of the early 1920s were made for headphones, the first loudspeakers arrived in 1925. They were first embodied as flaring horns in imitation of phonograph speakers, like the Burns, a 1925 model made of artificial tortoise shell. By 1927, such equipment was obsolete wherever there was electricity: powerful new models like the RCA Radiola 17 operated directly from AC house current. The age of modern radio had arrived. The authoritative machine or laboratory look of the battery radio gave way, in a mere decade, to the more liquid sculpture of Art Deco. The museum captures its very essence in a 1935, five-tube Sparton table model whose case is glass tinted a rich, smoky blue, a complex of planes and curves, the motifs of skyscrapers and sets for movie musicals. The radio has a companion piece: a General Electric clock set in a half-moon mirror, on chrome feet.

The 1920s and '30s were the age of radio, but the age of television was having birth pains. The museum has the evidence in one of the strangest, rarest devices in the communications collection: the Jenkins Optical Scan-

Opposite. The Atwater Kent Model II radio receiver of 1923 featured high-quality, molded Bakelite components mounted on a "breadboard." This four-tube, battery-powered set offered one stage of radio frequency amplification and two stages of audio amplification. Displayed with it here is an appropriate Burns loudspeaker, with an artificial tortoise-shell horn

Above. This 1936 Sparton Model 558 blue glass mirror radio, the quintessence of Art Deco, is admired for its "Century of Progress" styling. The five-tube superheterodyne receiver with a short-wave band was made by the Sparks-Withington Company

Opposite. A primal relic from the dawn of T.V., this is the prismatic disc optical scanner of Charles Francis Jenkins. In 1923, he used it to successfully transmit "radio vision." Four rotating prisms, geared around a central lens, formed a mechanical scanning forerunner to today's electronic scanning system

Above. Something of the pride, solidity, and skill of pre-World War I America is suggested by these two "railroad grade" Hamilton pocket watches of 1915–16

ner. With four glass rotating prisms or discs geared together around a central lens, the scanner was the actual experimental TV camera with which Francis Jenkins of Washington, D.C., successfully transmitted moving pictures for the first time. The date was June 13, 1923.

When one technology has been developed to maturity, we usually look around to find something new waiting to replace it. Thus in the nineteenth century's last decades, when coal- and wood-burning kitchen stoves had been essentially perfected, along came gas. But right on the heels of gas came electricity, with pioneering electrical stoves developing in the 1890s. Stoves fueled by kerosene appeared as well, to the special joy of rural housewives. Thus, early in the twentieth century, an unprecedented bonanza of choices was available. After 1915, when the application of thermostats rendered both gas and electric stoves miraculously automatic, it was clear that those two fuels would be the major rivals in urban kitchens.

A remarkable example of early electric stoves is the 1913 Standard, which manages to seem perilously topheavy and graceful as a lily simultaneously. In the Toledo-made Standard we see the basic black iron structure of the coal- and wood-burning stove, but ridiculously slenderized, as if announcing that massive fireboxes, grates, and ash dumps were forever eschewed. Perched high above the soaring burner surface is the oven, suggesting a microwave oven of the 1980s. Those attuned to the interdisciplinary links of fashion may see, in this extraordinary range of 1913, the same lines favored then in women's clothes: skirts pinched to a narrow hobble at the ankles, voluptuous curves in the torso, vast towering headgear.

No such fripperies of design mark the 1923 Westinghouse combination electric and coal-burning range. Massively practical, ready for anything, it was unusual, for by 1923 the standard kitchen range was a slender-legged creation in pale porcelainized finish, a style applied to both electric and gas. Often the color scheme was three-tone, with white, pastel gray, and black. Typical of the era is the Tappan range in the museum's marvelously authentic re-creation of a 1930 kitchen, a setting that inevitably strikes middle-aged and elderly Americans with nostalgia. Every artifact in the room is familiar: the graniteware pots on the stove, the porcelain-topped kitchen table, the cabinet with its slide-out work surface and flour dispenser, the small electric appliances, the boxes of prepared domestic products with labels picturing young housewives with bobbed chestnut hair. In preparing the 1930s kitchen, the Ford Museum reached into the collective heart of Americans over fifty, and found common memories.

The kitchen's refrigerator, with its stacked mass of cooling coils, reminds the same fiftyish visitors of the relatively brief history of electric-powered cooling. Nearly everyone who can remember the coil-crowned refrigerator also recalls when the family next door still used an icebox. By then the ice-

Above. An important transition in washing machines is represented by a c. 1875 hand-powered rocker scrub board, and the pioneering electrified Thor, made c. 1907 by the Hurley Manufacturing Company of Chicago

Right. Americans past age fifty may find the museum's Kitchen of 1930 a hauntingly nostalgic sight

box had subsided into a blue-collar bluntness from its grander years, and was routinely located on the back porch.

Electric refrigerators usually remained in the kitchen or pantry. Manufacturers made design changes with extraordinary speed in the 1930s, registering a sequence of contemporary styling themes. Consider the 1938 streamlined Norge, crisp and complacent in black-and-white porcelain and torpedo-shaped hinges, echoing contemporary cars and skyscrapers. The advertising copywriter's skill had already triumphed over the engineer's straightforward thesaurus, and such words as "hydrovoir" and "rollator" burst upon the 1930s housewife who, late in the Great Depression, was lucky enough to take delivery of such a marvel.

The 1930s kitchen displays common denominators of the time, and moves us by its familiarity. But as always, the era had its advancing edge of style and technology, far ahead of the crowd, and some interesting dead ends as well. Both characteristics spring ebulliently from a 1930 electric stove in the domestic arts collection. Like some odd but successful grafting of stove technology and Art Deco styling onto a Duncan Phyfe pedestal table, the Detroit-made Electrochef is graceful, elegant, and lonely among others of its time. Its space-wasting shape was doomed by the grubby necessity of pots and pans storage. A monument to uncompromising aesthetic tenacity, the twin-ovened Electrochef is—if the word can be applied to kitchen stoves—a classic.

In the world of washing machines, the early twentieth century delivered a pair of welcome electrically powered new mechanisms: a vertical container with an agitator, and a horizontal cylinder that revolved. First operated by hand, the washers soon were fitted with electric motors. Roller wringers, which had been around since before the Civil War, were bolted on, and the modern washer had arrived. The museum's formidable 1907 Thor Number One is a true pioneer of the breed. And Thor pioneered again in the early 1930s, electrifying the wringer.

Many early labor-saving devices, such as the hand-pumped vacuum cleaner, demanded almost as much human energy as they saved. One of the museum's supreme examples is the 1910 Rochester hand-cranked dishwasher, a truculent-looking wooden hopper lined with galvanized steel, its viscera bristling with coiled wire fingers to clutch the dirty dishes.

Difficult as it was to use, the dishwasher was on the right track. Elsewhere in the museum's encyclopedic domestic collection are entire evolutionary cycles which, like that of the dinosaur, simply ended when their time expired. We are amazed to learn how much effort and ingenuity our ancestors put into keeping their feet warm. A parade of foot-warmers from the eighteenth and nineteenth centuries made life more bearable for such outings as carriage and sleigh rides, for beds, and for such public gathering places as church, which was often unheated. A few footwarmers lasted into the early days of automobiles.

Many other domestic relics are more familiar to the modern eye. Some, like iron bread toasters from the days of hearth cooking, at least have modern counterparts. So do flatirons, and certain mashers and graters. A sense of discovery comes with discerning the gradual change in style that marked new generations of the same product; noting, for example, how early twentieth-century aluminum cookware—a new development—unnecessarily imitated the massive castings of its iron forebears.

Recently, the museum added a pioneering 1957 microwave oven, an unusual break with its general rule of ending the collections with 1950, and attesting to the revolutionary importance of microwave cooking. For in truth, as the artifacts show, most of today's kitchen appliances have been around for a while. Electric stoves have served us for about eighty years, electric waffle irons since 1918, and toasters since 1909. Westinghouse introduced an electric frying pan in 1911.

"Bathing did not become commonplace in America until the nineteenth century," snaps the text from a museum stanchion. Small wonder it even caught on then, for the collection of bathtubs hints more of torture chamber than toilette. The brave bather's first choice was between a copper-made product combining a horse trough and a coffin, and a tottery-looking tin basin that emulated an inverted sombrero. Other creative designs followed; most were merely aids to sponge bathing, not relaxing immersion. When the full power of Victorian innovation focused on bathtubs, however, the results were unspeakable. One of the most popular was a folding tub with its own hot water heater. Some folding tubs, arrayed for action, looked uncomfortably like guillotines. The main trouble was that tubs were waiting for the general introduction of indoor plumbing with hot running water. That occurred around the turn of the twentieth century, by which time the general conformation of future bathtubs (and flush toilets, perfected in the 1890s) had been clearly determined. The shape of the future shows in the museum's 1894 copper, wood, and zinc bathtub made by R. M. Wilson of Rome, New York. To harbor such welcome new appliances, space quickly was made for a separate room, the *bathroom*. By 1910, porcelainized fixtures were the norm, and the modern bathroom was in place.

As American homes waited for Thomas Edison to invent the phonograph, they were not bereft of mechanical music players. The music box, an ancient device wherein delicate metal fingers are plucked by the turning of cylinders or discs, produced sounds of marked beauty and delicacy. An assortment of automatic pianos provided similar repertoires. One elaborate alternative was the Violano Virtuoso, which combined automatic piano with a violin. Probably the favorite toward the end of the nineteenth century, and well into the twentieth, was the Regina, made in Rahway, New Jersey. Resembling the china cabinets of its time, the Regina was cased in Renaissance revival style, "especially suitable for use in the dining room," and some models played as many as twelve discs automatically with one

Opposite, top. The Standard electric stove, patented in 1913, reveled in a new slenderization made possible by eliminating the firebox. But it could not quite break with the construction features of its wood- and coal-burning predecessors

Opposite, bottom. The Borg-Warner Corporation of Detroit made this Norge electric refrigerator in 1938

Above. Around the turn of the century, the folding bathtub with attached water heater served homes lacking indoor plumbing. Such devices were being offered as late as 1920

winding—about half an hour's worth of music, not bad for the turn of the century. It would be many years before any phonograph could equal it. A Regina Type 35 in the museum collection dates from c. 1912; the model's heyday was 1900–1907, though some were made as late as 1920.

*L*ike a dream of Midwestern yesterdays, the blue-shuttered, pale yellow home of Wilbur and Orville Wright evokes an Ohio nostalgia almost powerful enough to mask the house's historical significance. New in 1870 when bought by the Wrights' father, it sheltered the famous brothers through much of their lives and, moved to Greenfield Village from Dayton, remains as it was when modernized by the young Wrights around the turn of the century, the point where it would be forever fixed in time. Thus the comfortable, weatherboarded house retains that precise era when its owners successfully experimented with flight. Original even to the window curtains, it is probably the most authentic of all Greenfield Village's historic buildings. Yet the house transcends its connection with famous former owners and becomes a three-dimensional text that explains, vividly and instantly, urban American home life of the 1900–1910 era.

Above all, the Wrights' eight-room house demonstrates the final triumph of the consumer society. It is a mass-produced household, beginning with the structure itself, a "balloon" frame building made of standardized lumber, and by framing and trim techniques agreed on by carpenters nationwide. All the furnishings, appliances, and housewares inside were factory made. Indoor plumbing, a porcelain-lined kitchen sink, aluminum cookware, linoleum on the floor, an icebox, and an arsenal of such labor-saving gadgets as the Bissell carpetsweeper made life easier for the Wrights and their housekeeper. Significantly, the men who designed one of history's greatest technological revolutions revealed their strong conservative bent by deciding against electric light in their 1903 modernization. They felt more comfortable with that old reliable, gas. The Welsbach mantles produced a splendid illumination, and gas enabled the Wrights to upgrade their heating apparatus conveniently and economically. They designed and built gas-burning fireplace units, surrounding each with stylish tan ceramic tile.

In 1904, the year after their first flight at Kitty Hawk, the Wrights brought the first running water into their home. The pump they installed at the kitchen sink recalls the brothers' modest plunge into indoor plumbing, ultimate proof of a twentieth-century household.

The Wright Cycle Company is now just next door. If the home of Orville and Wilbur seems an unlikely domestic cover for the fathers of flight, their technological and manufacturing springboard defies understanding. Did the air age truly begin in this drab, dim shop behind a southern Ohio store? The answer, as we have seen, is complex, but generally yes. Give the Montgolfier brothers their due. Properly credit fellow Frenchman Henri Giffard's

Opposite. Modern aviation was born in this shop, originally in Dayton, Ohio. Here, between 1897 and 1907, Orville and Wilbur Wright manufactured, sold, and repaired bicycles. They also designed and built early gliders and planes, including the historic craft that flew at Kitty Hawk, North Carolina, in 1903

powered dirigible. Recall Thaddeus Lowe, soaring over the popping muskets of Virginia's battlefields. Do not forget Germany's brave Otto Lilienthal, fatally injured in a glider wreck in 1896, the same year that Dr. Samuel Langley of Washington, D.C., earned little but ridicule for successfully flying his powered models. Yet having made appropriate bows to those and other pioneers, we must always give the prize to two young, provincial bachelor brothers from Dayton, the first to fly a manned, powered, heavier-than-air machine.

Almost alter egos in their interests and abilities, the Wrights mastered printing and photography before opening their bicycle business in 1892, when Wilbur was 25, Orville, 21. They began by retailing and repairing the bicycles of other manufacturers, but by 1896 they introduced the first of their own models, the Van Cleve. An original Wright Van Cleve bike is displayed in the shop today. (The St. Clair displayed on the museum concourse is the only Wright-made St. Clair known to exist.)

Reading of the experiments of the late glider Lilienthal, the Wrights dreamed of flying while thriftily attending to business. Their new passion was tempered by an intensely methodical approach, an innate sense of scientific caution that led them to weigh—and, in general, find wanting—the day's meager fund of information on flight. In 1900, after experimenting with kites and small gliders, they began building gliders designed to carry a pilot aloft. To study the unknown science of airfoils, they modified one of their bikes to carry a free-rotating third wheel, mounted horizontally on the handlebars. On the wheel, in turn, were mounted fragile metal flaps. Pedaling furiously around Dayton, the Wrights gathered their own data on airfoils by observing the movement of test surfaces.

By late 1901, the brothers had built their first wind tunnel, testing nearly fifty airfoils and in one year making the leap from bike-technology research to the very symbol of aeronautical research laboratories. Meanwhile they determined that the broad, oceanfront beaches of Kitty Hawk, North Carolina, offered the optimum qualities of steady wind and soft, treeless sand. In 1903, they built their fourth flying machine, and equipped it with a four-cylinder engine and two pusher-type propellers. With all the benefit of hindsight, we can accept as inevitable the events of December 17, 1903, when 32-year-old Orville Wright clattered aloft in their kitelike contraption. The flight remains etched in drama and surprise nevertheless, a deed stunning and brave and poignant. In all the history of invention and technology, is there a more imperishable image?

True, the world took little note at the time, a reaction disappointing to Orville and Wilbur. The Dayton newspaper ignored their first flight (although the Norfolk, Virginia, press rendered good—if inaccurate—coverage). But the Wrights were not of a kidney to be deterred by public indifference. Rapidly improving their fragile flyers, the brothers were in demand in Europe by 1908. French and German companies purchased Wright

Opposite. For more than forty years, this 1870 house was the Wright family home in Dayton. Wilbur died in the house in 1912 of typhoid fever. In 1938, the home and shop were moved to Greenfield Village under the supervision of Orville

Above. Orville (left) and Wilbur Wright, on the front porch of their home in Dayton, around 1910

airplanes, and so, at last, did the U.S. Army Signal Corps. The Wrights incorporated their own manufacturing company in 1909, the same year Dayton finally threw a gala for its famous native sons. In 1912, still living in the family home, Wilbur died of one of the time's implacable scourges, typhoid fever. Orville persevered, founded the Wright Aeronautical Laboratory, and invented the automatic stabilizers that would guide World War II dive bombers. In 1937–38, he helped Henry Ford move the old home and shop to Dearborn.

Like the Wrights' home, the shop seems to capsule the very air of 1903. In the back of the showroom, the brothers' office desk, chair, and typewriter reflect the foursquare probity that marked their owners. In one of the shop's back rooms, where bicycles and airplanes were made, is a reproduction of the original wooden wind tunnel. The first one had been destroyed, but Orville provided information that allowed Henry Ford's staff to reproduce it.

Orville, founding father, elder statesman, airman of the dawn, lived on to 1948, into the age of jets.

By 1909, the year of the Wrights' home-town recognition, no heavier-than-air manned craft had yet flown across the English Channel, although more than 120 years had passed since the first balloonist soared across. The London *Daily Mail* decided to incite flyers to a Channel conquest by offering a $5,000 prize. Among the contestants was Louis Bleriot of France, who had already prospered as the inventor of an automobile searchlight, and whose new passion was building airplanes. He had already survived several crashes, but he gamely took off again in his little monoplane, which bore an odd resemblance to a dragonfly. A mere three hundred feet above the fog-shrouded waves, without instruments, Bleriot throttled his three-cylinder Anzani engine against stiff winds and completed the crossing in thirty-seven minutes. It was the first international airplane flight.

In 1909, Louis Bleriot was first to fly across the English Channel, completing the world's first international flight. The daring Frenchman flew a plane of his own design and manufacture, and it was the virtual twin of this other 1908 Bleriot in the museum

The fragile little Bleriot that is the museum's oldest airplane is nearly identical to the one that flew the Channel, and was built by Bleriot in the same year, 1909. Its combination of metal fuselage panels with open wood framework, and the shape and positioning of its black fabric wings and tail, reveal the transition period from the original Wright flyer era into the beginnings of more modern-looking aircraft. The sequence continues in the museum's 1915 Laird biplane used by pioneer woman flyer Katherine Stinson; a 1916 Standard J-1, forerunner of the World War I "Jenny"; and a 1917 Curtiss "Canuck," a Canadian version of the "Jenny." The Curtiss is a rare survivor of more than ten thousand of its kind made in World War I. The first aircraft to be controlled by a stick, the model went on to become a popular barnstormer, air-mail carrier, and the first plane fitted with skis.

As the founding impulses of modern aviation gathered strength in the 1920s, another generation of legendary planes took charge. The museum's 1919 Curtiss Flying Boat, or Seagull, was the first commercial flying boat. Its maker, Glenn H. Curtiss, was another bicycle manufacturer who made a swift transition to aircraft; in 1910, he made the first landing on water, and pioneered landings and takeoffs on Navy ships before there were aircraft carriers. In 1919, Curtiss began manufacturing the famous Seagull, which that summer launched regular flight service between San Pedro and Santa Catalina Island, in California. The museum's example has a fifty-foot wingspan, and is powered by a Hispano-Suiza V-8 of 150 horsepower. A larger version made the first transatlantic flight, in 1919.

Even more renowned were the trimotors of the 1920s. First came the 1925 craft built in Holland by A. H. G. Fokker, and promptly flown by him to victory in the first Ford Reliability Tour. Subsequent Fokkers, made in

Opposite. "Flivver" had the potential for success as a light, simple, inexpensive personal airplane. But the crash of a similar plane and the death of its pilot so affected Henry Ford that he cancelled the project

Above. In this 1925 Fokker, the first trimotor ever built, Lieutenant Commander Richard E. Byrd made the first flight over the North Pole

Holland and New Jersey, completed the first California-to-Hawaii flight, the maiden international flight of Pan American Airways (Key West to Havana), and Amelia Earhart's transatlantic flight to Ireland. But the original Fokker Number One, the very craft displayed in the museum, participated in a still more breathtaking news event of the Roaring Twenties: famed explorer Richard E. Byrd's first flight over the North Pole, piloted by Floyd Bennett, May 9, 1926. Byrd, then a Naval lieutenant commander, named the ship "Josephine Ford" after the daughter of Edsel Ford, who helped finance the flight.

Another historic trimotor is the museum's 1928 Ford (the "Floyd Bennett") that carried Byrd, now a rear admiral, on the first flight over the South Pole, in 1929. The craft was powered by two wing-mounted Wright Whirlwind engines and a cowl-mounted Wright Cyclone. With their characteristic corrugated skin and plain-Jane profile, Ford Trimotors became a beloved, dependable craft around the world for many years. Almost two hundred of them were built at Dearborn from 1925 to 1932 in a building that still stands, adjacent to the museum and village.

Dwarfed by such relatively large planes is a little-known Ford airplane of the 1920s that might have changed aviation history, had it not been for a tragedy that nipped its development in the bud. True to his colors as a manufacturer of affordable transportation machinery, Henry Ford decided in 1926 to build an experimental, one-seat, low-winged monoplane. The resulting twenty-five-foot-wingspan, 550-pound "Flivver," looking a bit ahead of its time in design, was piloted aloft in Dearborn in July 1926 by Harry Brooks. Less than two years later, Brooks attempted a new light plane endurance record in another Flivver, but crashed in the Gulf of Mexico and was killed. Henry Ford, deeply affected by the loss of his pilot, canceled the Flivver project. The only surviving example is the original prototype, looking as though it could still buzz eagerly into the sky.

The year 1927 was a milestone in the history of commercial flight. A fleet of twenty-four Boeing biplanes commenced the nation's first regularly scheduled transcontinental passenger and mail service. It was a stop-and-go process, as the Boeing 40-B2 had a range of only 350 miles, cruising at 105 miles per hour. The pilot sat exposed to the elements in an open cockpit about midway in the fuselage; two passengers with sufficient courage could be crammed into a cabin between the pilot and the earsplitting Pratt & Whitney radial engine. The museum's specimen, proudly original down to the "United Air Lines—Coast to Coast" on its battered flanks, flew the Chicago-to-San Francisco leg of the historic schedule.

Only one year later, a significantly more modern craft was introduced by Lockheed. The Vega I quickly won acceptance by such pilots as Wiley Post, Amelia Earhart, Billy Mitchell, Charles Lindbergh, and Jimmy Doolittle; in such hands it won more long-distance records, over land and sea, than any comparable craft. Partial plywood construction cut down on the Vega's

Opposite. The Lockheed Vega was a pace-setting craft, and was the favorite of record-seeking pilots and explorers. Moreover, it was one of the first successful commercial airliners. The museum's example dates from 1929

Above. Designed in 1935, the Douglas DC-3 became the backbone of commercial aviation, and many examples were still flying in the 1980s. This one was built in 1939, and logged almost 85,000 flying hours before finally retiring to the museum in 1975

202

weight, and surprisingly modern instrumentation allowed a pilot to "fly blind." The museum's handsome example dates from 1929; it survived a long career as an airliner, and was used in Arctic exploration. It is restored today in the white-and-maroon colors of a forerunner of Continental Airlines.

As an airliner, however, the Vega was soon upstaged by that great workhorse of the air, the DC-3. Created by Donald Douglas in 1935, it singlehandedly ushered in the age of modern commercial aviation, and its design is reflected even in the jetliners of today. The museum's representative is a special one: built in 1939, it logged 84,875 flying hours in a thirty-six-year career with Eastern Air Lines and North Central Air Lines, a world record when it retired. In a flight history equaling twenty-five round trips to the moon, the airplane consumed 25,000 spark plugs and wore out 136 engines.

The homeliest aircraft in the collection is also one of the most significant. Resembling a soapbox racer grafted onto a giant electric fan, the original 1939 Vought-Sikorsky helicopter was the first practical "chopper." The designer was Igor Sikorsky, one of aviation's true originals. In World War I he pioneered building big, four-engine aircraft in his native Russia. Migrating to the United States in 1919, he designed and manufactured a famous flying boat, the S-42 China Clipper. Sikorsky had worked on the helicopter principle since 1919; twenty years later, he triumphed with a fabric-covered, open-cockpit craft called the VS-300. In 1943, Sikorsky took this very helicopter to Dearborn, and presented it to Henry Ford on a brilliant blue October day.

Edsel Ford had died only six months before, and Henry had resumed the presidency of the company. He had never relinquished the reins of the museum and village. But while the old tycoon was there to greet Sikorsky, he had named Henry II, his grandson, to make the official acceptance speech. Young Ford referred to the obstacles Sikorsky had encountered developing the helicopter as "the fires that temper men's determination." He called the strange craft "one of the marvels of our time."

Sikorsky's test pilot, C. L. Morris, put the craft through some stunts for the crowd as a Ford-built B-24 Liberator medium bomber rumbled high overhead on a test flight. The helicopter descended with one wheel touching a handkerchief on the ground, then hovered with a wheel cupped in a mechanic's hand, and finally, with a spear that protruded from the helicopter's nose, the pilot Morris—like a jousting knight—impaled a suspended iron ring. Someone pointed out the bicycle basket also mounted on the nose, and Sikorsky said he used that to carry his lunch.

He'd seen transportation collections all over the world, the inventor said, but this was the best, and it was a privilege to present "his little machine." Then he took it for a final ride, and the helicopter fluttered down for the last time on a lawn beside Village Road.

Opposite. Last flight of the first helicopter: Igor Sikorsky presented his historic craft to the Henry Ford Museum in 1943

Acknowledgments and Credits

*t*he combined Henry Ford Museum and Greenfield Village—The Edison Institute—is one of my favorite spots on earth. But glad as I was to begin a new book on the world's greatest indoor-outdoor museum, the work would never have been completed without the support and cooperation of the institute's curatorial and administrative staffs. Deprived of their expert guidance, I would surely have lost my way. What an embarrassment of riches the museum and village fling before any observer! Building a coherent narrative order for that vast collection of treasures was a challenging and sometimes frustrating assignment, demanding the sifting of thousands of artifacts, the study of complex interpretive programs, and the tracing of The Edison Institute's own evolution across the years. Fortunately, as I say, I had the benefit of skilled counsel, as well as friendly encouragement. Among the curators who generously shared their expertise were John Bowditch (power and shop machinery), Donna R. Braden (home arts), Nancy Bryk (textiles), Robert Cheyne (horology), Peter Cousins (agriculture), Robert E. Eliason (music), Steven K. Hamp (archives), Randy Mason (transportation), Donald W. Matteson (communications), Larry C. McCans (guns, toys, photography), Christina H. Nelson (ceramics and glass), Walter E. Simmons II (metals), and director of collections Kenneth M. Wilson (furniture). Special thanks go to Candace T. Matelic, manager of interpretive training, Ed Merrill, manager of interpretive programs, and John L. Wright, director of education. G. Donald Adams, director of marketing and public relations, and Peter Logan, of the institute's media relations department, helped in a thousand ways. President Harold K. Skramstad, Jr., rendered enthusiastic aid and encouragement throughout the project. Harold Sack, president of Israel Sack, Inc., of New York City, obligingly shared his rare personal recollections of Henry Ford as antiques collector. At my publisher's, senior editor Joan Fisher was a skilled and steadfast ally from the project's beginning, and helped chart its course; she and Sheila Franklin also guided me through dangerous thickets of gist and syntax. Finally, for support both practical and inspiriting, my thanks to the companion of all my journeys: Gwen C. Wamsley, my wife.

James S. Wamsley
Richmond, Virginia

Opposite. The wicker picnic basket on this 1904 Model L Packard is a carryover from those used on horse-drawn coaches in the days of elegant al fresco dining

All photographs are by Ted Spiegel except for those on pages 29, 34, 36, 38, 40, 44, 46–51, 56–58, 60, 64, 70, 72–3, 94, 97, 101, 108, 116, 124, 130, 132–34, 137, 140, 144–48, 150, 152, 156, 158, 160–62, 164–65, 167–69, 172–79, 181–83, 187, 190 (top), 191, 195–99, 201–2, which are reproduced courtesy the collections of Greenfield Village and Henry Ford Museum, Dearborn, Michigan

Index

Numbers in italic indicate illustrations

Abbott, Anne, 129
Ackley Covered Bridge, *14*
Acme automatic bar machine, 183
Affleck, Thomas, 42
Agnew Eagle, 99
airplane collection, 130, 135, 197–203
Albany cutter, 97, 99, *101*
Alcobuilt Schenectady passenger locomotive, 179, *180*
Alexander, William, 49
Allen, J. Lathrop, 85
alto horn, 85
Amati, Nicolo, 57
Ambler, Enoch, 88
"American blouse," 125
American Dictionary of the English Language, An, 62, 63
American Eagle Bank, 130
"American flip-flop" hay rake, 48
American La France, 177
American long rifle, 89, 90
American truck, 163
amethyst flask, 75
Anglo-Irish style cut-glass pitchers, 76, *208*
Apperson Jackrabbit, 171
appliances, 122, 125, 186–91
arc lamps, 107
Arkwright, Richard, 35
armchair, *41, 43*
Armington and Sims Machine Shop, 105, 109, 113, 114–15, 119
Armstrong, Edwin H., 185
Art Deco, 185, *185*, 190
"Art Garland" stove, 122, *123*
Artillery Mechanical Bank, 130
Atlantic cable, 95
Atwater Kent Model 10 radio receiver, *184*, 185
Atwood, William Hooker, 163
Austin, W. W., 148
automobile collection, 27, 143, *147*, 148–51, *152*, 153–77

automotive dealerships, 177
Autoped, *178*

*B*aldwin, Matthias W., 136
banjo, *84*
Banjo clock, *54*
banks, 130
"Barber vase," 129, *130*
baritone horn, 85
Barlet elbow melodeon, 85
bar machine, Acme automatic, 183
barshare plow, 37
bassoon, *56*
bathtubs, 191, *191*
beer wagon, 136–37
Bell, Alexander Graham, 113
Bennett, Floyd, 201
Bennett Tower, 214
Benz, Karl, 149
Benz Velocipede, 149
Best Friend, 101
Bible, 25
bicycles, 99, *101*, 141, 143, *144,*
    145, 146, 147, 177, *192, 193, 195*
"Big Mike," 138
Billings, Andrew, 55
bipolar dynamo, Edison, 109
Bissell carpet sweeper, 125
blanket chest, *64,* 67
Bleriot, Louis, 197, 199
Bleriot mono-plane, *196–97, 197,*
    199
blockfront desk, 42
Blue-backed Speller, 65
Boeing 40–42, 201
boilers, *32,* 33
bones (musical), 84
boneshaker, 141
book and document collection, 25,
    27
bookcase, 42
boots, 73

boring mill, 35
bottle collection, *6–7,* 51, *75–77,*
    78–79
Boulton, Matthew, 33
box stove, freestanding, 67
box telephone, 117
bracket clocks, 55
Brady, Mathew B., 97, 128
brass and German silver tuba, 85
brass instruments, 83
"breadboard, the," 185
breechloading muskets, 91
Brewster and Carver chairs, 41
Brewster George IV phaeton, 137
Brewsters, 137, *140*
Bridgeport milling machine, 183
"britannia," 81
Brooks, Harry, 201
brougham carriage, 137
Brush, C.F., 107
Bryant, Clara Jane, 157
buggies, 137
bugle, keyed, 83
Buick, David Dunbar, 166
Buick Model F, 166
Burbank, Luther, 19, 181, 183
Burns radio, 185
buses, 166
butchers' wagon, 136
Byrd, Richard E., 201

*C.*H. Brown & Co. engine, 105
Cadillac, *2–3,* 167, 169
calculators, 117
calico cotton, 55, 71
camera equipment, 97, 117, 119
camera obscura, 97
Campbell, Angelica, 39
card table, 42, 65
Carey jointer, 113
carpeting, 73
carpet loom, 73

carpet sweepers, 125
Carr, James, 128
carriages, horse-drawn, *36, 39,*
    136–38
cartes de visite, 97
cartridges (bullets), 91
Cartwright, Edmund, 35
Carver, George Washington, 20
Case traction engine, 121–22
Cayley, George, 130
ceramic heating stove, 45
ceramics collection, 49, 128–29
chairs, *40, 41, 41, 42, 42*
chair table, *40, 41*
chariot, horse-drawn, *36, 39*
Chesapeake & Ohio Allegheny
    coal burner locomotive (Big Al),
    181, *181*
chest(s), *41, 42*
Chevrolet, Louis, 169
Chevrolet Baby Grand, 169
Chevrolet Royal Mail Roadster,
    166, *168,* 169
china, 128–29
China Clipper, 203
Chinese plates, 49
Chinese porcelains, 49, *50, 51*
Ching-teh, chen tea service, 49
Chippendale-style chairs, *42, 43*
Chippendale-style clock, 55
Chippendale-style furniture, 42–44
Chippendale-style highboy, *45*
Chrysler, Walter P., 172
Chrysler Corporation, 172
Chrysler Imperial landau, 172, *174*
Chrysler parade car, *152*
Cincinnati Milling Machine of
    1881, 113
Civil War era bottles, 77
clarinet, *56, 83*
Clemens, Samuel, 96
Clinton, De Witt, 77, *100, 101*
clock collection, *54, 55, 86, 214*
clock movements, 87

clock shop, *23, 26*
clothing, 55, 57, 73, 125
Clymer, George, 95
coaches, horse-drawn, 39, 97,
    136–38
coal-burner locomotives, 181, *181*
coal-burning stoves, 186
cobalt slip decoration, 75
coffeepots, silver, 52
Cohen, Mrs. D., 20
Cole Brothers engine, 99
Colt, Samuel, 91
Columbia Electric, *160, 163*
Columbian press, *94, 95*
column and cornice clock, 86
combines, Massy-Harris, 183
communications collection, 113,
    117, 185–86
compote, *77*
comptometer of Felt and Tarrant, 117
Concord coach, 97
Conestoga wagon, *38, 39,* 41
cook stoves, 68, 69–70
cookware, 71
Cooper, James Fenimore, 89
Cord, E.L., 172
Corliss, George Henry, 103
Corliss engines, 103, *105*
cornet, valve, 83
Cotswold Cottage, 45
cotton, 73
cotton calico, 55, 71
cotton gin, 55, *61*
coupe, 39
courthouse, 20, 23
covered dish, 77, *208*
creamware pottery, 51
crinoline cage, 125
crock, 75
Crolius inkwell, 75
cup plate, 77
Curie, Eve, 19
Currier and Ives lithographs, 27
Curtiss, Glenn H., 199

Top. Early and middle nineteenth-century American pitchers

Lower left. Covered compote by Gillinder & Sons called "Westward Ho"

Lower right. Cut-glass pitchers from England (left) and Pittsburgh, Pennsylvania (right)

Curtiss "Canuck" (airplane), 199
Curtiss Flying Boat, 199
cut-glass pitchers, *76, 208*

D. S. Pillsbury Collection, 83
Daboll carpet sweeper, 125
Daguerre, Louis J.M., 96
Daguerreotype, 96, 97, *97*
Daimler, Gottlieb, 149
Danforth, Josiah, 81
Davenport, Thomas, 93
Davy, Humphrey, 93
decanter, 77
deep-dish, 75
Deere, John, 86, 88
de Forest, Lee, 185
delftware, 51
De Palma, Ralph, 171
desks, 42
"Detroit Electric," *160*, 163
Detroit Racing Club, 157
Diesel, Rudolf, 105, 107
Diesel engines, 105, 107
Diesel locomotives, 179, 181
dirigibles, 130, 135
dishes, 75, 77
dishwasher, 190
Doble (steam car), 149
Dodge touring car, 172
doglock, 59
dolls, 130, *131*
domesticity, cult, 71
Douglas, Donald, 203
Douglas DC-3, *201, 203*
Doyen, The, 57
Downes, Ephraim, 214
Draise, Karl von, 99
Draisine, 99, *101*
drinking bowl, silver, 52
drug jar, 51
Duesenberg, Fred, 172
Duesenberg Model A, 172
Duesenberg Model J, 172

Duesenberg (1931), *173*
dump wagon, 137
Duncan Phyfe pedestal table, 190
Duncan Phyfe piano, 86
Dunlop, John, 143
Durant, William C., 137, 166, 169
Duryea, Charles, 151
Duryea, J. Frank, 151
Duryea (car), *150*
Dutch fan, 119

E agle Tavern, 20, *22, 23*
earthenware, lead-glazed, 73, *74*
Eastlake, Charles, 128
Eastlake-style icebox, 128
Eastman, George, 117, 119
Eby, Jacob, 55
Eddy, G.W., 67
Edison, Thomas Alva, 17, 97, *97*,
    169, 175
  death, 20
  inventions, 111–12
  life of, 107, 109
Edison bipolar dynamo, 107
Edison electric pen, 117
Edison Illuminating Company
    building, *107*, 109, 112
Edison Institute, dedication, 19
Edison Institute buildings, 17–23,
    45, 47
"elbow melodeon," 85
electrical stoves, 186, 190, *190*
electric cars, 163
electric motors, 93
electric refrigerators, 190, *190*
Electrochef stove, 190
electroplating, 81
Empire Organ Co., 85
Encyclopedie (Diderot), 25
English guitar, 57
"English square action," 86
Eureka mowing machine, 121
Evans, Oliver, 96

Top left. Oak armchair from Massachusetts, c. 1650–80
Top right. New England maple armchair, c. 1700–25
Lower left. Queen Anne chair, c. 1750
Lower right. Chippendale chair, c. 1755

ewer, porcelain, 129
Expert Columbia, 141, 143, *144*

*F*abric collection, 55, 57, 71, 73
Fairbottom Bobs, *32*
Faraday, Michael, 93
farm equipment collection, 37, 86, 88–89, *118*, 119–21, *120*, 181–83
farm steam engines, *120*, 121
fashions collection, 55, 57, 125
Federal mahogany clock, 55
Federal radios, 185
Fetch, Tom, 161
fiddle, *84*
Field, Cyrus, 93, 95
fife, 56
firearms collection, 59, 61, 89–93, *91*, *92*
fire bucket, pitch-doubled, 49
fire engine (toy), 130
fire fighting equipment, 48, 49, 98, 99, *99*, 138, *139*, 177
fire hose, 49
fireplaces, 45, 47
fireplace stove, Franklin, 66, 67
Firestone Lincoln, 171
five-plate stoves, 45
flageolet, 56
flasks, 51, 75
Fleming, John A., 185
Fletcher, J.C., 69
flintlock fowler, 61
Flivver, *29*
"Flivver" monoplane, *198*, 201
"Floyd Bennett" (airplane), 201
Fokker, A.H.G., 199
Fokker Number One, *199*, 201
Fokker trimotor plane, 199, *199*
Ford, Clara (wife of Henry), 23
Ford, Edsel, 171–72, 175, 203
Ford, Henry, 20, 23, 24, 33, 65, 143, 149, *156*, 177, 181, *182*, 196, 201
  birth, 157

career, 159–61
  early life, *154*, 157
  education, 157
  marriage, 157
Ford, Henry, II, 203
Ford, William, 157
Ford "Arrow," 159
Ford B-24 Liberator Bomber, 203
Ford Dearborn Township farmhouse, 23, *154–55*
Ford Fordor sedan, 167
Ford Franklin sedan, 175
Fordmobile, 159
Ford Model A, 159, 172, 175
Ford Model K, 159
Ford Model T, 15, *165*, 166–67
Ford Model T touring car, 27, *29*
Ford Motor Company (Mack Avenue Building), 159
Ford "999," *158*, 159
Ford Quadricycle, 15, *157*, 159
Ford racer, *156*
Fordson Number One, 181, *182*, 183
Fordson tractor, 181, *182*, 183, *183*
Ford Trimotors, 201
Forster, Stephen, 85
Forsythe, Alexander, 91
Forsythe pistol, 91
Fort Meyers laboratory, 19, 112
fowler, 61
Franklin, Benjamin, 37, 45
Franklin fireplace stove, 45, 66, 67
freight wagons, 38, 39, 41, 137, *142*
"friendship" quilt, *70*, 73
furniture collection, 24–25, 40, 41–42, *43*, *44*, 45, 65–67, 127–28

*G*alvanometer, 95
Gardner, Alexander, 97, 128
gas stoves, 186
General Motors, 166, 169
generators, 107
Germanic pottery, 75

German silver baritone horn, 85
Giffard, Henri, 130, 193
Gilbert, William, 37
Gilmore, Patrick, 83
glass bottles, 8, 51, 75–77, 78–79
glass, pillar molding, 77
glassware, 128–29
glazed earthenware, 73
Glidden, Carlos, 117
gold bugles, 6–7, 83
"golden-oak" furniture, 128
Grabowsky, Max, 175
grain reapers, 88–89
Grammatical Institute of the
    English Language, 63, 65
Gramme, Zename T., 107
grand piano, 126
Grasshopper beam engine, 96
Gray and Woods planer, 112–13
gristmill, tower, 35
Guarnerius, Joseph, 57
guitars, 57, 59, 85
guns, 59, 61, 89–93, 92

*H*adley chest, 41
Hall, David, 82
Hall, John, 91
Hall, Rhodolph, 82
Hall flintlock rifle, 91
Hall muskets, 91
Hamilton "railroad grade" pocket
    watch, 186, 214
hand-pumper, 48, 98, 99
hansom cab, 137
Harahan Sugar Mill, 121
Harland, Thomas, 55
Harley-Davidson Cleveland, 177
Harley-Davidson Excelsior, 177, 179
harmonicon, 85
harpsichord, 59
Harte, Bret, 96
Hatch, F.L., 137
hats, 73
Haynes, Elwood P., 151

Haynes-Apperson (motor car), 151
hay rakes, 88
haystack boiler, 32
Headman, Andrew, 75
heating stoves, 67, 122
Hedstrom, Oscar, 177
Heinz, H.J., 20
Heinz home, 20
helicopters, 202
Henry, Joseph, 93
Henry rifle, 91, 93
Henson, William, 130
Hepplewhite clock, 55
Hepplewhite desk-bookcase, 62, 65
Hepplewhite mahogany piano case,
    58, 59
Hepplewhite sideboard, 65
Hertz, Heinrich, 185
highboy, 42, 44, 45
Highland Park factory generator, 25
highwheeler, 141, 144
Hills, Medad, 61
Hitchcock, Thomas, 59
"hobby horse," 99
Hoe, Richard, 95
hog plow, 37
Hoover, Herbert, 19
horns (musical), 83, 85
horology collection, 23, 52, 54,
    55, 56, 86, 186
horse-drawn carriages, 18, 36, 39,
    136, 137
horse-drawn wagons, 38, 39
Howe, Elias, 71
hubcaps, 170
Hunneman pumper, 99
Hussey, Obed, 88
H & W motor car, 151

*I*cebox, Eastlake-style, 128
ice skates, 15
Indian (motorcycle), 177, 179
Indian (India) spinning wheel, 25
Ingersoll milling machine, 183

Ingersoll-Rand Diesel locomotives, 179, 181, *181*
inkwell, Crolius, 75
internal combustion engine, 149
Irish-made plate, 51
Isaac Fiske valve bugle, 85

J. S. and M. Peckham parlor stove, 67
Jack-in-the-Box, 130
Jackson, H. Nelson, 161
Jacquard, J.M., 71
Jacquard coverlet, 73
Jaeger rifle, 61
jamb stoves, 45
Janney, E.H., 135
jars, 51, 75
Jarves, Deming, 77
Jefferson, Thomas, 37, 57, 86
Jehl, Francis, 19
Jenkins, Francis, 186
Jenkins Optical Scanner, 185–86, *187*
Jervis, John B., 101
jewelry, mourning, 57, *57*
John F. Stratton alto horn, 85
John Mitchell plan of North America, 27
jointer, Carey, 113
"Josephine Ford" (airplane), 201
jugs, 75, *80*
Jumbo dynamo, *108*, 109

K ay, John, 35
Kendall, Edward (Ned), 83
Kennedy, John F., 172
Kentucky rifle, 59
kerosene lamps, 127
kerosene stoves, 186
Kinetograph, 112
Kinetoscope, 112

Kip, Jesse, 52
Kip Cup, 52
Kirckman, Jacob, 59
kitchen (1930), 186, *188–89*
Knabe piano, *126*, 127
knee breeches, 73
knickerbocker suit, 125
Krarup, Marius, 161

L aird biplane, 199
Lallement, Pierre, 141
lamps. *See* lighting and lamps
Langen, Eugen, 105
Langley, Samuel, 195
Lannuier, Charles Honoré, 65
lantern clock, 55
lathes, *34*, 35, 37, 112
laundry equipment, 127, 188, *190*
lead-glazed earthenware, *74*
Lee, Robert E., 49
Leland, Henry M., 167, 169
Lenoir, Etienne, 105
LeSage, George, 93
lever-action pistol, 91
Lewis, W.K., 75
Leyden jar, 37
lightbulbs, 19
lighting and lamps, 47, 49, 77, 93, 107, 127
Lilienthal, Otto, 135, 195
Lincoln, Abraham, 20, 23, 89, 128, *131*
Lincoln Continental, 169, 175, *176*
Lincoln rocking chair, *131*
Lincoln V-12 convertible limousine, 175
Lindbergh, Charles A., 175
Lockheed Vegas (airplane), *200*, 201, 203
locomotives, *4–5*, *100*, 101, *134*, 135–36, 179–81. *See also* railroads
locomotive (toy), 130, *133*

Logan County Courthouse, 23
log cabin, 65
"Long-legged Mary Anne," 109
Loomis, Samuel, 42
looms, 35, 71
Loranger, Gristmill, 105
Lord Fauntleroy suit, *124*, 125
Lowe, Thaddeus, 130, 195
Lownes, Joseph, 52
Lumière, Auguste, 119
Lumière, Louis, 119
Lycett, Joseph, 129
lyre clock, *54*

*M*achine tools, 34, 35, 112–13, 183
McCord, Susan, 73
McCormick, Cyrus Hall, 88
McGuffey, William Holmes, 20, 65
McGuffey, birthplace, *16*, 20
McGuffey home, 65
McGuffey Readers, *16*, *17*, 25, 65
McIntyre, Samuel, 65
McNamee, Graham, 19
Magic bank, 130
Manny's Patent Reaper, 88–89
"Mansion of Happiness," 129
mantel clocks, 86, 87
map collection, 27
Marconi, Guglielmo, 185
Marconi radio receiver and transmitter, 185
Marcus, Siegfried, 149
Marriott, Fred, 172
Martin, C.F., 85
Mason Fairlie locomotive, *4–5*
Massey-Harris combine, 183
matchlock, 59
Matthew, David, 101
Maudslay, Henry, 35
Maybury stove, 45
Menlo Park laboratory, *17*, 19, *19*,

102, 109–11, *110*
Mercer sport touring car, 171
Mercer Type 35 raceabout, 171
Mergenthaler, Ottmar, 95
metal-working lathes, *34*, 35, 37
Michaux, Ernest, 149
microwave oven, 191
millinery shop, 20, *21*
milling machines, 113, 183
mills, 35
Miner, Uzal, 83
Mission-style furniture, 128
Moravian pitcher, 75
Morris, C.L., 203
Morse, Samuel F.B., 93, 96
Morton, Herbert F., 23
motion pictures, 112, 119
motorcycles, *148*, 149, 151, 177
motor scooter, *178*
motor vehicles, 27, 121–22, *121*, 137, 143, *147*, 148–51
mowing machine, 121
Murphy, Charles ("Mile-a-Minute"), 143
musical instruments collection, 57–59, *58*, *60*, 81–86, *82*, *83*, *126*, 127
music box, 191–92
music collection, 27
muskets, 59, 61, 91
Mussechenbroek, Peter van, 37
Muybridge, Eadweard, 119

*N*ational Game Tourist," 130
New Bremen Glass bottle, 51
Newcomen, Thomas, 33
Newcomen steam engine, 33
Newsham, Richard, 48, 49
New Warrior mowing machine, *118*
New York reaper, 89
Niepce, Nicephore, 96
Norge electric refrigerator, 190, *190*

North, Noah, 61
Noyes, John, 51

*O*boe, 83
oil tank wagon, 137
Oldfield, Barney, 143, *158, 159*
Old Ironsides locomotive, 136
Old Number 90, 181
Old Pacific (Packard car), 161, *162*
Olds, Ransom E., 161, 163
Oldsmobile, *160,* 161
omnibus, *18*
opaque white glass, 75
ophicleide, 83
organ collection, 85
Oriten, 143, *146*
Otto, Nickolaus August, 105, 149
Otto engines, 105
Owens, Lane & Dyer steam
    engine, 121

*P*ackard, James Ward, 161
Packard, Model L, *204*
Packard, tan and black speedster,
    168, 171
Packard Twin Six, *168,* 171
Packard, William Dowd, 161
Papin, Denis, 31, 33
Parian eagle vase, 128
Parian porcelain vase, *129*
parlor stoves, 67, *67,* 69, 122, *123*
Parsons, Charles A., 105
"Patersons," 91
pearlware, 51
Pearson house, *4*
pedestal table, *190*
Peerless Victoria, *168, 169*
pewter, 81
Philadelphia highboy, *42, 45*
Philadelphia Public Ledger, 95

phonographs, 111, 112, 191, 193
photography equipment, 96–97,
    117, 119
Phyfe, Duncan, 65
piano collection, 58, 59, 81, 85,
    85, 86, 126, *127,* 191
pianoforte, 81
pie plate, 75
Pierce-Arrow "Great Arrow," *169*
Pierce-Arrow roadster, *169*
"pillar molding," 77
pint flask, 75
"Pioneer," *77*
pistols, 89, 91
pitchers, 51, 72, 75, 76, 77, *77,* 81, *208*
Pittsburgh decanter, 77
Pittsburgh glass tumbler, 77
Pittsburgh punch bowl, 77
planers, 112–13
plates, 49, 51
plows, 37, 86, 88
plumbing, 191, *191,* 193
Plymouth House, 45, 47, *47*
Plympton, Abigail, 45
Plympton, Thomas, 45
pocket watches, 56, *186*
Pope, Albert A., 141, 143, 163
Pope-Hartford, 163
Pope-Toledo, 163
porcelain(s), 49, *50,* 51, 77, 81, 129
Port Huron tractor, *119*
portrait prints, 97
"possible Delaware" clock, 55
pottery, 73–75
powder flask, 92
powder horn, 90
power machinery, 105, 107
President, The, 134, 135
printing presses, 95–96
Pullman, George, 179
Pullmans, 179
punch bowl, 77
Putnam Machine Company
    planer, 112

*Q*uadricycle, 15, *157*, 159
Queen Anne chair, 42, *42*
quilt collection, 73

*R*acing cars, 157, *158*, 159, 161, 171–72
radio receivers, 185, *185*
railroads, 19, *134*, 135–36, 179–81. *See also* locomotives
railroad coaches, 179
Railway Express freight wagon, *142*
Rapid electric car, 163, 166
Rapid trucks, *160*, 166
Rauch and Lang electric car, *160*, 163
RCA Radiola, 17, 185
reaper-binder, 121
Recamier Grecian sofa, 65
redward, 75
reed organs, 85
refrigerators, 186, 190, *190*
Regina Type 35 music box, 191–92
Reis, J. Phillip, 113
Remington, Philo, 117
Reuben Tower tall-case clock, 86
Revere, Paul, 52
Revere coffeepot, 52
Revere teapot, 52
revolvers. *See* pistols
riding chairs, 39
rifles, 59, 61, 89–93
rifle-shotgun, 92
Riker, Andrew L., 151
Riker truck, 151
robots, 183
Rochester hand-cranked dishwasher, 190
Rockefeller, John D., Jr., 19
rocker lap organ, 85
Rogers, Will, 19
Rogers 303-0 American Class locomotive, 135
Roper, Sylvester Hayward, 143, 149

Roper (car), 143, *147*, 148–49
Ross, William, 39
Rover, 143
Rudge rotary tricycle, *145*
Rumford roasters, 47, 49
rum jug, 80

S. S. Columbia, 109
S-42 China Clipper, 203
Sack, Harold (son of Isaac), 24
Sack, Isaac, 24
Salamandar Works, 73
Saltbox house, *46*, 47
salt-glazed stoneware, 51, 73–75, 80
Sam Hill (locomotive), 135
"Sandwich" glass, 77
Sarah Jordan Boarding House, 19, 111, *111*, 112
Satilla (locomotive), 135
Savery, Thomas, 33
schoolhouse, 20
Schurtz, A., 97
Scott, Grant, 89
screw-cutting metal lathe, *34*, 35, 112
scrub board, hand-powered rocker, *188*
Seagull (airplane), 199
Sears, Kate B., 129
Selden, George B., 149
serpent (musical instrument), 81
Seth Thomas clocks, 86
sewing machines, 71, 122, 125
sgraffito technique, 75
sharps carbine, *91*
Sheffield plate, 81
shoes, 73
Sholes, Christopher L., 117
shotguns, 61, 92
Sikorsky, Igor, 203
silverware, 51–52, *53*, 81, 83
Singer, Isaac, 71, 125

Architectural details in Greenfield Village

Sivrac, Comte de, 99
skid engines, 105
Skramstad, Harold K., Jr.,
    19–20, 23, 24, 25
Slater, Moses, 85
Slater, Samuel, 35
Slater's Mill, 35, 55
sleighs, 97, 99
slip decoration, 75
Smith, Horace, 91
Smith and Wesson, 91
Smith Creek railroad station, 19
snaphance, 59
Soap Hollow tall-case clock, 86
Society of the Cincinnati, 49
soft-paste bone ash porcelain, 81
soft-paste pitcher, 72
Soule, Samuel, 117
Sparton Model 558 blue glass
    mirror radio, 185, 185
spinning looms, 35
spinning wheel, 25
square piano, 85
stage coaches, 97
"stakes," 81
Standard electric stove, 186, 190
Standard J-1 (airplane), 199
Stanford, Earl of, 33
Stanley, F.E., 163–64, 172
Stanley, F.O., 164
Stanley, M.N., 69
Stanley eight-horse power model
    (1903), 164
Stanley Model 60 runabout, 160,
    164
Stanley Rocket, 164
Starley, James, 141, 143
Starlight stove, 17
steamboat (toy), 130
steam-driven generators, 107
steam engines, 23, 31–33, 32, 96,
    103–7, 104, 105, 115, 120, 121
steam locomotives, 181
steam-powered cars (steamers),
    163–64

steeple compound marine steam
    engine, 105
Stevens, Thomas, 141
Stiegel, Henry W., 51
Stinson, Katherine, 199
stoneware, 51, 73–75, 80
Stoney Creek Sawmill, 105
stove, Franklin, 67
stove collection, 17, 45, 47, 49, 66,
    67–71, 67, 69, 122, 123, 186,
    190, 190
stove, Troy, 67, 68
streetcars, 136, 137
Strowger, Almon B., 117
Stutz Bearcat, 171, 172
summer-winter fabric pattern, 73
Supreme Court furniture, 42
Swan, Joseph, 109
switchboards, 117

*T.*Gilbert & Co., piano, 86
tableware, 49–51, 128–29
Talbot, William H.F., 96
tall-case clocks, 54, 55, 86
tankards, 51, 52, 75
Tappan range, 186
Taws, Charles, 59
Taylor, Zachary, 95
teapots, silver, 52, 53
telegraph, 93, 95, 113
telephone, 113, 117
television, 185–86
ten-plate stove, 49
Terry, Eli, 55, 86
textbooks, 65
textile mills, 33, 35, 55
Thayer, Ephraim, 49
Thompson, Benjamin, 47
Thor Number One washing
    machine, 188, 190
Tiffany, Louis Comfort, 129
tin-glazed delftware, 51
tinware, 71

Tom Thumb, 101
tools, 17, 34, 35, 37, 112–13
Torch Lake (locomotive), 4–5
"tourist" vehicle, 175
toys, *10–11*, 129–30, *132, 133*
tractors, *119*, 121–22, *121*, 181–83
transfer-printed creamware, 51
Tribune Blue Streak, 143
tricycle, 143, *145*
Tripp Sawmill, 105
trousers, 73
Troy stove, 67, 68
trucks, 151, 166
trumpet, *6–7, 82*
tuba, 85
Tucker, William Ellis, 81
  china by, *72, 81*
typewriters, *116*, 117

*U*naimate robot, 183
utility jars, 75

*V*acuum cleaners, 125, *127*, 190
Vail, Alfred, 93
Van Dorn, Jacob, 52
Van Dorn, Maria, 52
Van Rensselaer, Stephen, 57
vases, 77, 128–29, *130*
Velo, 149
vests, 73
Victoria, 137, *140*
Violano Virtuoso, 191
violins, 57, 60, 84
Virginia, University of, 65
Virginia Housewife, or, Methodical Cook, The, 71
Volcanic lever-action pistol, 91
Volcanic Repeating Arms Co., 91
vote recorder, 111
Vought, Sikorsky 300 helicopter, *202, 203, 203*

W. Eddy screw-cutting lathe, 112
wagons, commercial, 136–37. *See also* trucks
waistcoats, 73
Walter, Thomas U., 128
Walker, W.H., 119
washing machines, *188*, 190
Washington, George, 49, 51, 129
Washington, Mary Ball (mother of George), 42
Washington camp bed, 25
Washington highboy, 42, *44*
Washington press, 95–96
watches, 52, *56*, 86, *186, 214*
watch shop, 23
watercooler, 80
Watson, Thomas, 117
Watson thumper, 117
Watt, James, 33, 55
Watt steam engines, 33
Wayside Inn (South Sudbury, Massachusetts), 17
Webster, Daniel, 99
Webster, Noah, 63–65
Webster, Rebecca, 63
Webster home, 20, *62*, 63, 65
Welsbach mantle, 127
Wesson, Daniel, 91, 93
Westinghouse, George, 109, 135
Westinghouse electric/coal-burning stove, 186
West Orange laboratory, 112
"Westward-Ho," 77
wet-plate camera, *117*
whale oil lamps, 77
Wheeler and Mellick thresher, 119
Wheelock, Mama, 41
wheelocks, 59
Whieldon, Thomas, 51
White, Peter, 89
White House china, 129
White House "Sunshine Special," 175, *176, 177*
White House vehicles, 137, 171, 175, *176, 177*

White Model G touring car, 164
White pistols, 89
Whitney, Eli, 61, 91
Whittier, John Greenleaf, 99
Whitworth, Joseph, 35, 37
Wilkin, Godfrey, 67
Wilkinson, John, 35
Willard, Aaron, 55
Willard, Simon, 55
William and Mary high chest of
    drawers, 42, 44
Wilson, James, 67
Wilson bathtub, 191
Winchester rifle, 93
windmill, 30
windowpanes, 77
Wingert rifle-shotgun, 92
Winton, Alexander, 153, 157,
    159, 161
Wintons (motor cars), 153, 157
Wise, John, 130
Wizard of Oz (first edition), 25
Wood, Calvin, 20
Wood, Jethro, 86
Wood, Walter A., 121
Wood and Caldwell pitcher, 51
woodwinds, 56, 83
woodworking tools, 112–13
Wright, E.G., 83
Wright, Orville, 19, 20, 193,
    195–96, 195, 197
Wright, Wilbur, 193, 195–96, 195
Wright Cycle Company, 192
Wright family home, 2–3, 20,
    193, 194
Wright St. Clair (bicycle), 195
Wright Van Cleve (bicycle), 195
Wright wind tunnel, 195, 196

Zouave jacket, 125

Menlo Park gate